Silk Ribbon Embroidery
a collaboration of artists from around the world

A compendium compiled by Di van Niekerk,
Annine van Reenen and Werner Etsebeth

Silk Ribbon Embroidery
a collaboration of artists from around the world

A compendium compiled by Di van Niekerk,
Annine van Reenen and Werner Etsebeth

As the intention of this book is to inspire, buyers of the book are allowed to use the ideas demonstrated in this book for their own personal projects. Copying for any commercial purposes whatsoever is not allowed under any circumstances.

Every effort has been made by the publisher to ensure that the information (photographs and text) in this publication are correct as supplied by the embroidery artists.

First published in 2013 by Dicraft Publishing

Copyright © Dicraft Publishing 2013

All rights reserved. No part of this publication may be reproduced, stored in a retrieval system or transmitted in any form or by any means, electronic, mechanical, photocopying, recording or otherwise, without the prior written permission of the copyright owners.

Publisher	Di van Niekerk
Editor	Annine van Reenen
	Werner Etsebeth
Photographs	Supplied by the Embroidery Artists themselves.

COPYRIGHT AND LICENSING

Title: A BEAUTIFUL PLACE
Artist: TC Chiu
Artist copyright © The Art Publishing Group licensed by Cypress Fine Art Licensing Union, NJ 07083, USA.

Titles: STOP AND SMELL THE ROSES, ORANGES AND BOUGAINVILLEAS, RED ROSE GARDEN and SUNFLOWERS AND WHITE ROSES.
Artist: Sharon Maia Wilson
Artist copyright © Sharon Maia Wilson 2012.
Licensing by Sharon Maia Wilson

Titles: BLUE BENCH IN ROSE GARDEN and WICKER CHAIR WITH COSMOS
Artist: Peter Motz
Artist copyright © Sjatin Art BV painting by Peter Motz 2012.
Licensed by Sjatin Art NV

Titles: OLIVE OWL and RED OWL
Artist: Cori Dantini
Artist copyright © Cori Dantini 2012. Licensed by Meehan Design Group.

Titles: TRANQUIL WATERS WITH BLACK SWANS, GIRL REACHING, SHADES OF SUMMER, COUNTRY HOUSE WITH PICKET FENCE and CHILDREN FISHING.
Artist: Andres Orpinas
Artist copyright © Andres Orpinas 2012. Licensed by Cypress Fine Art Licensing, Union, NJ 07083, USA.

Titles: FLEUR GATHERING FLOWERS WITH MANON and DANIELLE CUDDLING HER BABY CHICK.
Artist: Sarah Kay
Copyright © 2012 John Sands (Australia) Ltd.

All the above are licensed to Di van Niekerk's Crafts Unlimited.
Tel +27 (0) 21 671 4607 Email: di@dicraft.co.za Website: www.dicraft.co.za
P O Box 461, Howard Place, 7450, Cape Town, South Africa.
All rights reserved.

Title: ROSE SAMPLER
Artist: Verdi
Copyright © 2010 Verdi and Di van Niekerk's Crafts Unlimited.
Tel +27 (0) 21 671 4607 Email: pucketty@pixie.co.za;
Website: www.dicraft.co.za
P O Box 461, Howard Place, 7450, Cape Town, South Africa

Contents

Foreword   7

Part 1   8
BLUE BENCH IN ROSE GARDEN
Marina Zherdeva   10
Marina Kukuy   16

Part 2   18
A BEAUTIFUL PLACE
Tamara Sherstuk   20
Marie Mordue   22

Part 3   24
SHADES OF SUMMER
Leonora Roodt   26
Joey van Tonder   30

Part 4   32
TRANQUIL WATERS WITH BLACK SWANS
Nancy Leasure   34
Karin Leith   38
Margot Kerr   40
Annisa Lam   42

Part 5   44
COUNTRY HOUSE WITH PICKET FENCE
Leonie Arendt   46
Poorna Kularatne   50

Part 6   52
STOP AND SMELL THE ROSES
Olga Smirnova   54

Part 7   58
ORANGES AND BOUGAINVILLEAS
Larisa Torop   60

Part 8   64
RED ROSE GARDEN
Annamaria Kelly   66

Part 9   70
FLEUR GATHERING FLOWERS WITH MANON
Oya Altinkök   72

Part 10   76
DANIELLE CUDDLING HER BABY CHICK
Elena Lisovitskaya   78

Part 11   80
WICKER CHAIR WITH COSMOS
Valentina Ilkova   82
Ita van Heerden   86

Part 12   88
ROSE SAMPLER
Kristina Nilsson   90
Mania Badmagrian   96

Part 13   98
GIRL REACHING
Jane Stilgoe   100
Carol Bianconi   104
Claire Rubie   108

Part 14   112
OLIVE OWL
Lena Thiel   114
Marina Zherdeva   119

Part 15   120
RED OWL
Olga Smirnova   122

Part 16   126
CHILDREN FISHING
Nermin Ağridağ   128

Part 17   132
SUNFLOWERS AND WHITE ROSES
Franci Janse van Rensburg   134

Foreword

It does not matter where in the world you live. The value, inspiration and sheer pleasure gained from looking at the embroidery done by stitchers in far-flung countries is immeasurable. Needlecraft techniques are more or less the same the world over. It is the style that is different and, in so many ways, reflects the personality of the country that you are in. From the soft colours used by Australians, to the whimsical nature of Ukrainian crafts, the definitive design of the Russians, or the sheer elegance of French embroidery, artists are inspired by their heritage, their culture and the environment in which they live. By combining the work of silk ribbon artists from all over the world, this book is multi-cultural and inspirational. Each of the designs appear more than once and it is fascinating, in each case, to see how the different artists have interpreted what they had to work with.

All wrought with skill, the work of the 2012 Di van Niekerk Silk Ribbon Embroidery Competition winners that is featured in this book will inspire your own silk ribbon embroidery. It will give you the confidence to try things in your own way, tempting you onto greater works.

Because it is not an instructional book, it does not dictate. Instead, it will encourage you to take your own path towards satisfaction in your silk ribbon embroidery.

Hazel Blomkamp
Author and designer

PART 1

Blue Bench in a Rose Garden

Marina Zherdeva
Marina Kukuy

I worked the white Chamomiles in the middle, below the bench and in the basket, with French Knots. The white Peonies in the basket were done with loop stitches. I worked the basket with twisted silk ribbon.

Marina Zherdeva
Moscow, Russia

"Ribbon embroidery has captured me with its magic to transform a flat image into a three dimensional work of art. It brings the image to life at a glance – it's a miracle! It's the only kind of embroidery where volume is created by different materials such as silk ribbons. The best result is achieved with silk ribbons, and especially those hand dyed by Di van Niekerk. I just love them, they offer unlimited possibilities in colour variations and are so natural, so rich in colour, so life-like!

I took up embroidery as a hobby in 2010 along with my other hobbies – some painting, cross-stitching and thread painting during my childhood; and sewing and design at school. My most recent passion is photography. I've learnt about composition of a design and colour schemes; which I consider to be the most important factors when choosing a design to embroider, but my interest in flowers determines my choice of design in most cases.

What I love most in creative needlework is to combine different techniques and materials, other than just ribbons and threads, and achieve extraordinary visual effects. Every design I choose challenges me to find new ideas and new approaches to transform the picture into 3D bas-relief – that's real fun! Another admirable feature of silk ribbon embroidery is its simplicity and easiness to get a lovely piece after just a few stitches.

The charming scene, *Blue Bench in a Rose Garden* is a design with great 3D potential, lots of opportunities to make volumetric elements. I enjoyed each element of my embroidery!

STRAW HAT

Wrap a small piece of bowl-shaped plastic or tiny plastic container with thin plastic film. The film will help to detach the silk base from the plastic. Fix with an elastic band. Wrap a piece of silk organza over the hat ball to form a silk base and fix with an elastic band as well.

Apply glue stick on the top of the plastic, where the top of the crown is, and start a thread spiral just from the centre of the top. Work carefully but quickly as the glue dries fast. Make sure that every turn of the thread is firmly attached to the silk and to the previous turn. Apply glue around the circumference and lay turns until the crown height reaches 15mm. The crown is ready. Let it dry on the container. Do not cut the thread or remove the silk base and plastic film.

When the crown is dry, take the container away and carefully stretch the plastic film and silk base over the disk of cardboard, which works as our 'pent' and marks the edges.

As an option you may insert the bottom of the container through the small round cut-out on the cardboard (should go through with some effort) and stretch the plastic film and silk base over the cardboard disk, whatever is easier for you.

Apply glue around the circumference on silk and continue laying turns over this horizontal surface. Make sure that every turn of the thread is firmly attached to the silk and to the previous turn.

Make pent of desired width and cut the thread. When the pent is done and dry, remove the cardboard. Remove the film very carefully. Your thread should be stuck to the silk base in every point. Apply glue where needed on the reverse side of the hat. Fix the tail on the reverse. Carefully cut the excess of silk base. Try to avoid glue spots on the face side of the hat. You may leave the hat white or paint it with aquarelle pens according to the design. Please note that glue is sensitive to water and needs to be dried immediately if the thread gets wet.

AGAPANTHUS

Keep in mind the direction of sunlight on the design. Start to embroider on the left bottom part of Agapanthus and move towards upper right part.

Start with ribbon of dark colors underneath; mix darker colour with lighter colours and use mainly light colour ribbon on the upper right part of the plant.

Embroider mainly with reverse straight ribbon stitch. To add air to the Agapanthus leaves make some leaves connected with the design just by one end.

To prevent from fraying use transparent glue at the cut sharp leaves edges.

Stems

Use thin bead wire and green stranded cotton for each stem. Make each stem with 10cm of wire and 20cm of green stranded cotton.

Make a small loop on a piece of bead wire and attach a length of thread to it with a knot. Pass the full length of the thread through a glue stick and wind around the wire, moving the wire by fingers clockwise or anti clockwise – whatever is convenient for you. Make sure the turns of the thread lay tight together, gently pushing the turns with your finger. The wire should not be visible. Fix the end tail of the thread with glue and allow to dry.

Make another small loop at the start end of the wire again for better fixing in the ball and insert it into the Agapanthus ball.

Agapanthus flower heads

These flourishing balls are made separately. Stretch silk organza in the hoop and draw a 32mm-circle with a sharpened, soft-leaded pencil or fine fabric marker. This diameter equals to 2 diameters of the ball painted on the design (d=16 mm). Cover 32 mm-circle fully with loop stitches. Make French knots (each of 2 turns) with a thread in the middle of each loop stitch. Seam around the circle, leave thread tails. Cut out the circle, leaving 3–4mm of organza. Add some synthetic fuzz, pull off the thread tails and make a ball, hiding the organza edges inside. Insert the seam into the ball. Tie the thread in a knot, hide or cut the tails. Buds are made in the same way as the Agapanthus balls, but their diameter equals to 20 mm, and the circle is filled with loose French knots.

The Rose bushes with yellow-pink and white roses were done with left or right ribbon stitches and French Knots in the centre. The leaves were done in straight and ribbon stitches.

The petals of the white Peonies on the bench are done with white silk ribbon and the stamens with yellow thread.

The pot with pink geraniums is worked with long and short stitches.

The grass below the bench and next to the pot are worked with stranded silk. The grass above the walkway, around the Chamomiles, is worked with stacked straight stitches with stranded silk thread.

Dark colours are embroidered first, below the lighter colours, with straight and ribbon stitches.

HOSTA SHRUB

Stems and flowers
For the Hosta stems, use 0.3mm bead wire and light green wool thread. The stems of the Hosta are made a bit differently than those for Agapanthus.

Pull only 5–6cm of a tail of the thread through a glue stick. Wind it around the wire, covering 2.5–3cm of the wire length to fix this layer on the wire.

Continue to spin the wire, but the thread should go over the first layer towards the beginning and should be free of glue. This is the second layer and forms the soft media to embroider the Hosta flowers. When you reach the beginning, continue to spin and make the third soft thread layer, go to the end of the wire, fix the tail with glue. Now you have 2.5–3cm of thick soft thread layer and can easily embroider Hosta flowers.

Work the two upper rows of smaller flowers with 2mm silk ribbon and the bottom rows of larger flowers with 4mm silk ribbon.

Leaves
Hosta leaves are made of 2 ribbons. The top layer is green, and the bottom layer is white.
Apply glue (from a glue stick) on the white ribbon and let it dry.

Outline a leaf with a marker on the green ribbon and apply glue on the reverse side. Quickly cut out the green leaf.

Put the green layer over the white ribbon and spread it. Cut a 2–3mm edge around the white ribbon leaf background using the edges of the green leaves as a guide. Shape the leaves and let it dry.

Make all the leaves and spread them in accordance with the design.

You may embroider the leaves if there is a tail, or just sew them as appliqué."

Marina Kukuy
Russia

"I was stunned by the beauty of Helen Eriksson's embroidery. It seemed very difficult to me. I have collected Di van Niekerk's books and began to learn to embroider through them. I am the owner of the Network Design Studio. I apply embroidery on curtains for decoration, interior decoration and clothing. I get inspiration from everywhere: books, advertisements, landscapes and landscape designs of my students. My dream is to get a new book by Di van Niekerk with the author's signature."

PART 2

A Beautiful Place

Tamara Sherstuk
Marie Mordue

Tamara Sherstuk
Nakhodka, Russia

"I live in Russia in the city of Nakhodka. It has always been my dream to learn cross-stitch, but when I saw ribbon embroidery, I liked it very much and decided to learn how to sew with ribbons. Valentina Ilkova taught me how to and she showed me a book of Di van Niekerk, *Volume Embroidery Encyclopedia*. This book has helped me to learn more about the different methods of ribbon embroidery. My source of inspiration is my favourite flowers. I have flowers in lots of colours. I grow them all year, winter and summer. I chose to embroider A *Beautiful Place* because it reminds me of my garden.

I loved the chairs and to embroider them with threads in the art surface, Salvia flowers embroidered in ribbons are very similar to real garden flowers. I made a small pillow on the chair in engineering needle weaving. Red roses on the bushes are very small and made with twisted ribbon."

Before I started on my picture I studied it closely, getting an idea of the colours and materials I would be using.
I did the pillars first, using my sewing machine. I placed thin batting behind the printed fabric and outlined the pillars with the 'stitch-in-a-ditch' technique used by quilters.

Between the umbrella and the pot with flowers I added plant stems and did seed stitches for the tree tops.

For the background at the top behind the umbrella I used seed stitches and I tried to match the stranded cotton to colours on the fabric as close as possible. It gives depth and a feeling that you want to walk through the garden.

For the pot with the pink flowers I used soft colours for the flowers at the bottom and around the pot.

For the lollipops (round green shrubs in the front) I did French knots. This was a challenge. I did the dark spots first. I used a dark cotton as shading. The next colour is fern or apple green and lastly lemon green for the highlight spots.

Tip: Take a photo of trees and work from there using the colours and shading as a guide."

Marie Mordue
Dundee, KwaZulu Natal
South Africa

"In 2005 I saw a picture of a chair with a hat and flowers at a friend's house. It was very pretty. Must say I have never done embroidery and wasn't really interested at all, but that picture got me going. My friend gave me my first picture, *Floral Vista*. I went for a couple of lessons and was hooked. I ordered a picture transfer from Di, *Shades of Summer*. I also ordered a DVD on one of Di's workshops, and since have never looked back. I love my garden – it is my inspiration. I buy any garden magazine and trees are my passion – all the shades of green in one tree. I wanted my trees to look like that. I do the same with flowers. I love playing with colour. I have done about 28 pictures, most of them from Di. Billy, my husband, is also involved selecting frames and backgrounds for my finished pieces. All glory and honour to my Lord and Saviour.

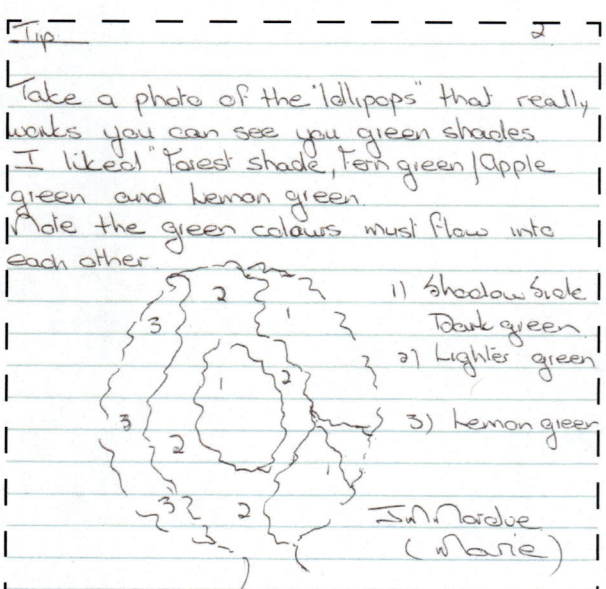

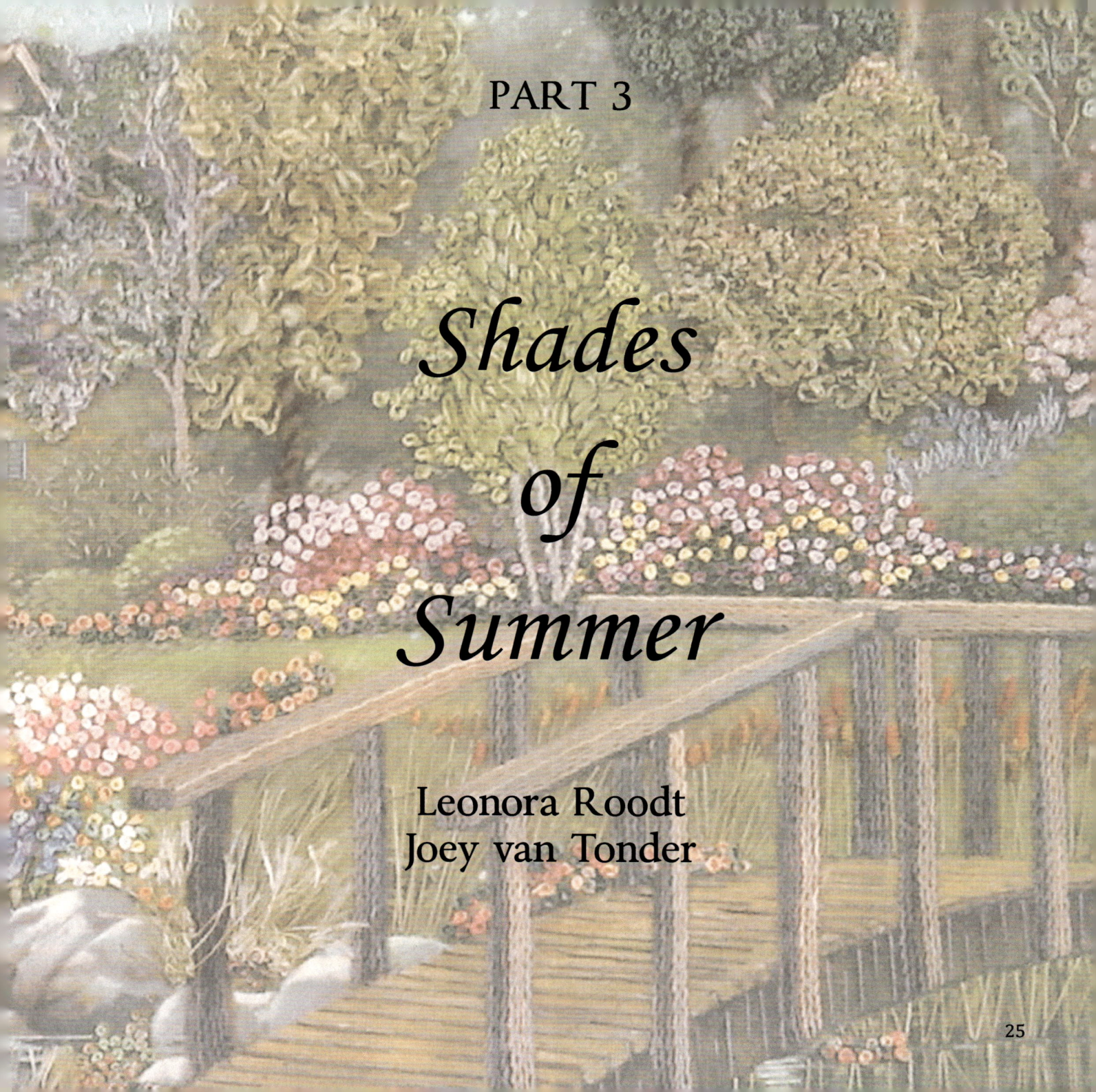

PART 3

Shades of Summer

Leonora Roodt
Joey van Tonder

Leonora (right) and Rabia Motala

Leonora (right) and Mathilda Roodt

Leonora Roodt
Bergbron, Gauteng
South Africa

"I became passionate about ribbon embroidery about six years ago after chatting to a family member, Mrs Mathilda Roodt, who has become a very dear and special friend of mine. She introduced me to her 'teacher', Mrs Rabia Motala, a Muslim lady who resides in Ridgeway and since March 2007 I started going to classes on Saturday mornings. Initially it was only going to be for a year just to learn all the different types of stitches and techniques but it didn't work out that way!

I am still going to classes and enjoy every single minute of it! If I am unable to go, I get 'withdrawal symptoms'. I get my inspiration from Rabia and fellow class friends. I am fortunate to be one of her pupils as she is brilliant and generous in sharing her knowledge of the various stitches and techniques with all of us. Her embroideries are masterpieces and there is nothing that can't be done in all the years that I have been going to her.

It is 'therapy' for us to sit together and share our ups and downs whilst embroidering. Di van Niekerk's comment on her website: "Embroidery is good for the soul", is absolutely correct!

I have a wonderful supportive family who allow me to go to my 'therapy' classes. I also help my husband at his work, so spare time is somewhat limited but I try to make the most of it.

SKY
Use a stranded thread of cotton and work feather stitches with lazy daisy stiches and French knots in between. Fill the lower section with seed stitches.

TREE TRUNK
Work the tree trunk on the left of the scene with stranded cotton wrapped with one strand. Work the branches with stem stitches using one strand. Couch the bouclé yarn with one strand of cotton.

THATCH ROOF
Fill the roof with straight stitches using French ribbon and the top of the thatch with stem stitches using one stranded thread. Work the bottom end of the thatch with tight French knots, one wrap, using two strands of cotton and working the stitches close together.

WATER AND MOSS ON ROCKS
Use metallic thread and stitch over the rocks to create the water reflection, adding stitches in the pond areas. For the growing moss, work seed stitches with French ribbon.

REEDS
Work the thin stems in long stitches couched with some fly stitches. Work the leaves in straight, twisted stitches and stitched in place with a stranded thread.
Work the reed flowers with ribbon using French knots, one wrap, and add some golden seed beads in between the French knots.

TREE NEXT TO BIG HOUSE
Fill the tree trunk with rows of stem stitches, whipped with perlé thread. Work the branches with stem stitches as well. The foliage or leaves are filled bouclé yarn couched with a stranded thread.

BULRUSHES AT BRIDGE
Work the stems in long fly stitches and the tops in bullions; then fly stitches underneath. Use stems stitches for the reflection of the bulrushes in the water. Work short stab stitches for the tops.

FLOWERS

White flowers
Work the petals with inverted stab stitches and fly stitches for pointed petals using silk ribbon. Add French knots for small flowers. Work the centres using small balls from wool fibre/roving stitched in place with stranded thread.

Yellow flowers
Work the petals with French knots and inverted stab stitches. The centres are red-brown seed beads stitched in place with a strand of cotton.

Blue flowers
Work the petals with silk ribbon using puffy stitches and French knots, one wrap. The centres are made with French knots using two strands of cotton.

Red flowers
Work French knots, two wraps.

LEAVES
Use silk ribbon and work French knots and inverted stab stitches.

ROCKS
Trapunto the rocks in the foreground."

Joey van Tonder
Bethlehem, Free State
South Africa

"Since 2005 I've embroidered several of Di van Niekerk's beautiful kits. I've done this project, *Shades of Summer*, in my own style. I keep myself busy with knitting and crochet, but I find ribbon embroidery quite relaxing and enjoyable.

Work the branches in the top left corner with fly stitches and blossoms in ribbon stitch using white, blue and green silk ribbon. The orange flowers below the tree are worked with silk ribbon using French knots. Add some green knots in between. The leaves of the dark green tree are done with ribbon and the tree trunk with bouclé thread. The purple sky is worked with fly stitches and extended French knots. The trees behind the house are done with French knots. The roof, doors and windows are worked in long and short stitches. The foliage of the yellow-green tree in front of the house is worked with loose French knots and the tree trunk with bouclé thread. The foliage of the pale green tree in front of the house is worked with fine French knots. The white and orange flowers under the tree are worked with French knots and the stems with stem stitches.

Work the foliage and branches of the tall trees on the right with bouclé thread. Work the leaves in between with French knots and fly stitches. Work the foliage of the light green tree to the left with French knots, single wrap. The dark pink blossoms on the shrub-like tree on the right are worked with French knots, one wrap.

The top of the handrail of the bridge is worked with French ribbon using long and short stitches. The walkway and balustrades of the bridge are worked with long and short stitches using stranded thread.

The purple, orange and maroon flowers above the wooden bridge are also worked with French knots.

The rocks at the water edge are worked with long and short stitches. White thread is used for the highlights on top of the rocks.

The grass in the bottom left corner of the scene is worked with split stitches, while the thicker part of the grass is done with long and short stitches. The seeds are worked with clusters of French knots.

For the flowers at the bottom, use purple and pink ribbon, and thread, making French knots. The tall white flowers are worked with gathered ribbon stitched onto the surface.

The tuft of grass is worked in split stitches, using single stranded thread.

The larger flowers in front are worked with silk ribbon.

The waterlily leaves on the water are worked with long and short stitch."

PART 4

Tranquil Waters with Black Swans

Nancy Leasure
Karin Leith
Margot Kerr
Annisa Lam

Nancy Leasure
Seminole, Florida
United States of America

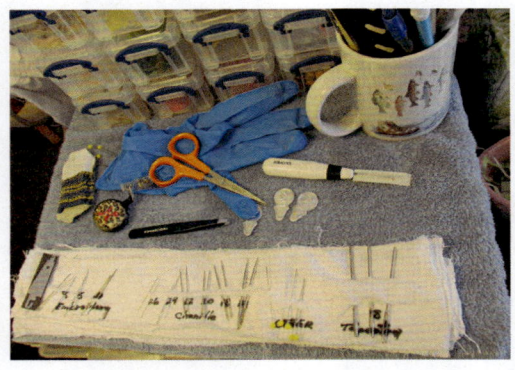

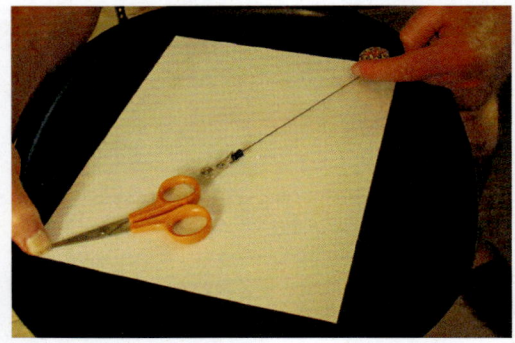

"I became passionate about ribbon embroidery after I became disabled and had to quit working following a car accident. Since I was nearly housebound, I tried numerous crafts to help fill up my time. After many failures of interest (left-handed people have to be really talented to figure out knitting, and counted cross stitch nearly made me blind!); I came across a copy of Di van Niekerk's Ribbon Embroidery and Stumpwork. I couldn't find any store in the U S where I could order the sampler and supplies, so I went online and ordered directly from her. I was instantly hooked on silk ribbon embroidery and never looked back. It's always challenging and there's always a new and different spin you can put on a project. I make sure every time I repeat making a particular piece, that the second one is way better than the first.

Occasionally, for personal use only, due to copyright restrictions, I will use a photo from a magazine as inspiration for a piece. And, because I live near the Gulf of Mexico, I'm beginning to work with a local artist to develop beach scenes (houses, birds, vegetation and flowers) for sale to the local tourist population. I can do ribbon embroidery, but I can't draw or colour!

I chose the *Tranquil Waters with Black Swans* because I saw it had the potential to pull me right into the picture. I wanted to bring it to life so it could do that for others too, and doing that developing perspective, was what I enjoyed most about making it. I also loved making the black swans!

I was really drawn to this particular project because of its quiet beauty and peaceful atmosphere. I happened to make one version well before I decided to make a second to submit into competition. That first one taught me a lot about what changes I wanted to make to the competition submission.

To start with I ordered an extra ribbon pack with the kit, not because there is insufficient ribbons supplied with the kit, but because my desire, especially for landscapes, is to provide an extra luxuriant background of flowers and vegetation; and in this case, I wanted to provide lots of colour.

Using the correct ribbon for the black swans was very important to me. In nature, the female bird is not as colourful as the male, so in this case, I treated the swan in front as being the male.

In making his feathers, I often started with a ribbon stitch, but then pulled it all the way through to leave a little extra volume to the feather. This technique was enhanced by the extra saturation of the ribbon's colour, which made it stiffer than the usual supple, pliant silk ribbon.

The necks of both swans were done in a combination of black and grey silk thread.

I also used red thread for the face and beak and left the white stripe bare.

I decided to stitch the tree line at the horizon in a light purple thread using tiny seed stitches. I just followed the vertical shapes of the trees, without addressing the branches. In adding that touch, it lent more perspective to the piece.

Making this change, however, covered up the third flying bird, so I repositioned it.

The next thing I did was to make notes about the order in which I wanted to embroider the piece. I do this because I'm left-handed, and find it's often useful to re-order the steps to accommodate that. I don't want to be dragging my left hand through work that was designed for the right-handed world, but primarily because I like to combine steps wherever I can safely do so. The designs of the trees on the left and right sides of this piece are similar and could be done at the same time without jeopardizing the quality of the work. This allows me to use the same threads, wool and ribbons without interruption, providing a consistent look.

I tried several treatments for the white trees before deciding which thread to use in stem stitch and then go over the trees again using metallic blending filament.

I always keep a spare small hoop close at hand for trying out things such as this, and also various types of stitches to see what will work best for a particular piece.

And by the way, if my first stitch when starting up a new ribbon is to be a ribbon stitch, I go ahead and simply make a small stab stitch before covering it up with the ribbon stitch. Too many times I've lost that first ribbon stitch because I accidentally stretched it a tiny bit too much while making the next stitch or some such mishap. By anchoring that first stitch right away I don't need to worry about it.

Then, after preparing the piece for embroidery, using a zig-zag stitch around the perimeter of the panel and its backing, putting it into the frame, unwrapping the ribbons and threads and putting them into my storage system, I checked over all of my supplies and especially my needles to see if any needed to be replaced. Di is right; needles have to be replaced after every 2–3 major projects. They get dull and are often bent. I made sure I had all of the supplies I needed, and ordered any I was missing. Another of my idiosyncracies is that I usually keep one large and two other, smaller projects going at the same time, so if there's a delay in one piece, or if I just need a break from it, I have one or two others to fall back on. I get cranky if I don't do at least some embroidery every day."

Karin Leith
Pretoria

"I am a Chartered Accountant and lecture at the University of Pretoria, so my embroidery hobby would seem to be at odds with this! I have been embroidering for a number of years, starting out with cross stitch and since then have tried my hand at gold work and creative embroidery with amazing support from various talented and patient teachers. I did this piece under the guidance of a very special person, Viv Trent from Flowers & Thyme Embroidery Studio in Wapadrand. She coaxed and cajoled me through the piece and was an amazing source of inspiration, so a very special word of thanks to Viv. Until doing this piece, I had done almost no ribbon embroidery at all, so it was a daunting and challenging project and many times I felt somewhat overwhelmed. However, as the ribbons and threads that we chose to use slowly brought the embroidered piece alive and the flowers, leaves and trees took on a life of their own, I realised why I really enjoy this creative art form. As a keen gardener myself, it was an opportunity to paint my own garden with lots of colour and texture. My inspiration comes from seeing other beautiful finished pieces and believing that I could also do something like that."

39

Margot Kerr
Pretoria

"I am always intrigued with the gradual transformation from a flat colourless picture into a rich vibrant picture with many textures, colours and hues.

Annamaria Kelly and I became friends at work where she sometimes teaches me ribbon embroidery during lunch hour. She invited me to her home where I saw the exquisite embroidered pictures on walls throughout her home. She invited me to classes she held.

Annamaria is my inspiration, making embroidery fun, and her help and amazing ideas on how to use ribbon and other materials bring out the best in a picture. I chose the *Tranquil Water with Black Swans* because I felt that the combination of trees, water, flowers and the swans would be a challenge to do and would give me immense satisfaction."

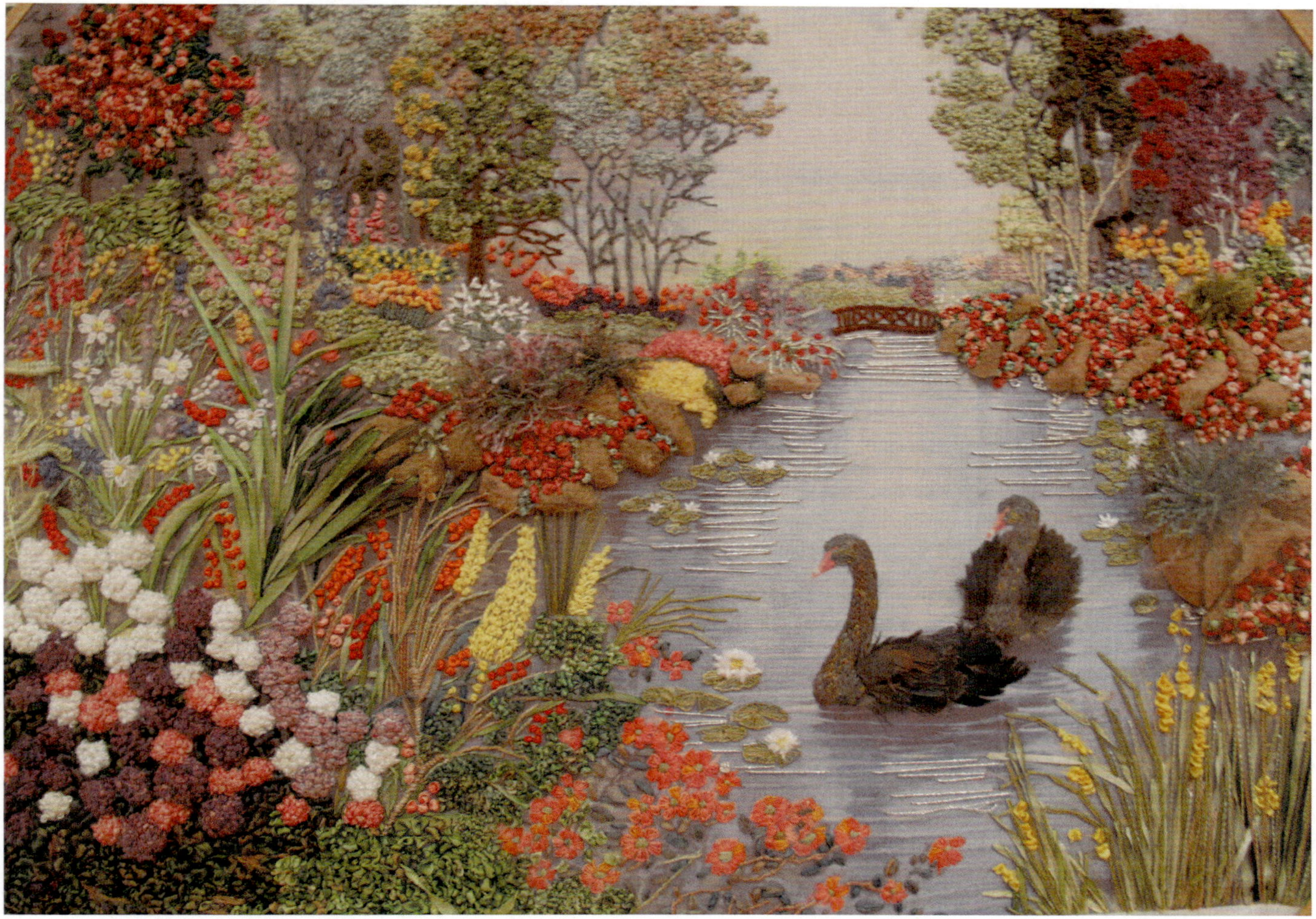

"I live in Hong Kong but my first experience in embroidery dated back in 1998 during the period of stay in New Zealand. I was fascinated by this beautiful form of art and over the years I dedicate most of my time to pursue into unbound limit in the world of embroidery .

I love all forms of embroidery and the early stage of my work are mostly pure stitching. It was until I came across Di's beautiful range of ribbons and products which divert my attention to explore further into the realms of ribbon works. Since then, I have developed a growing passion in ribbon embroidery and stumpwork .

Unlike pure stitching which requires regularity, neatness and precision, ribbon is relatively 'uncooperative'. I enjoy most about ribbon embroidery as it has no set rules, leaving me free to experiment , manipulate and tame. The simple stitches could produce eye catching and stunning results.

I have chosen *Tranquil Waters with Black Swans* because it is such a delightful scene containing plenty of elements which offers excellent opportunities for the interpretation of texture and perspectives to the whole landscape . I applied a combination of ribbons, texture threads , wooly fibers , water soluable fabric, hessians, handmade rocks to the embroidery piece to create dimensions and textural effects.

I have been teaching embroidery for over 10 years now at my studio, Dancing Needles. It is so enjoyable to share my knowledge and experience with people who have the same passion in stitching."

Annisa Lam
Hong Kong

43

44

PART 5

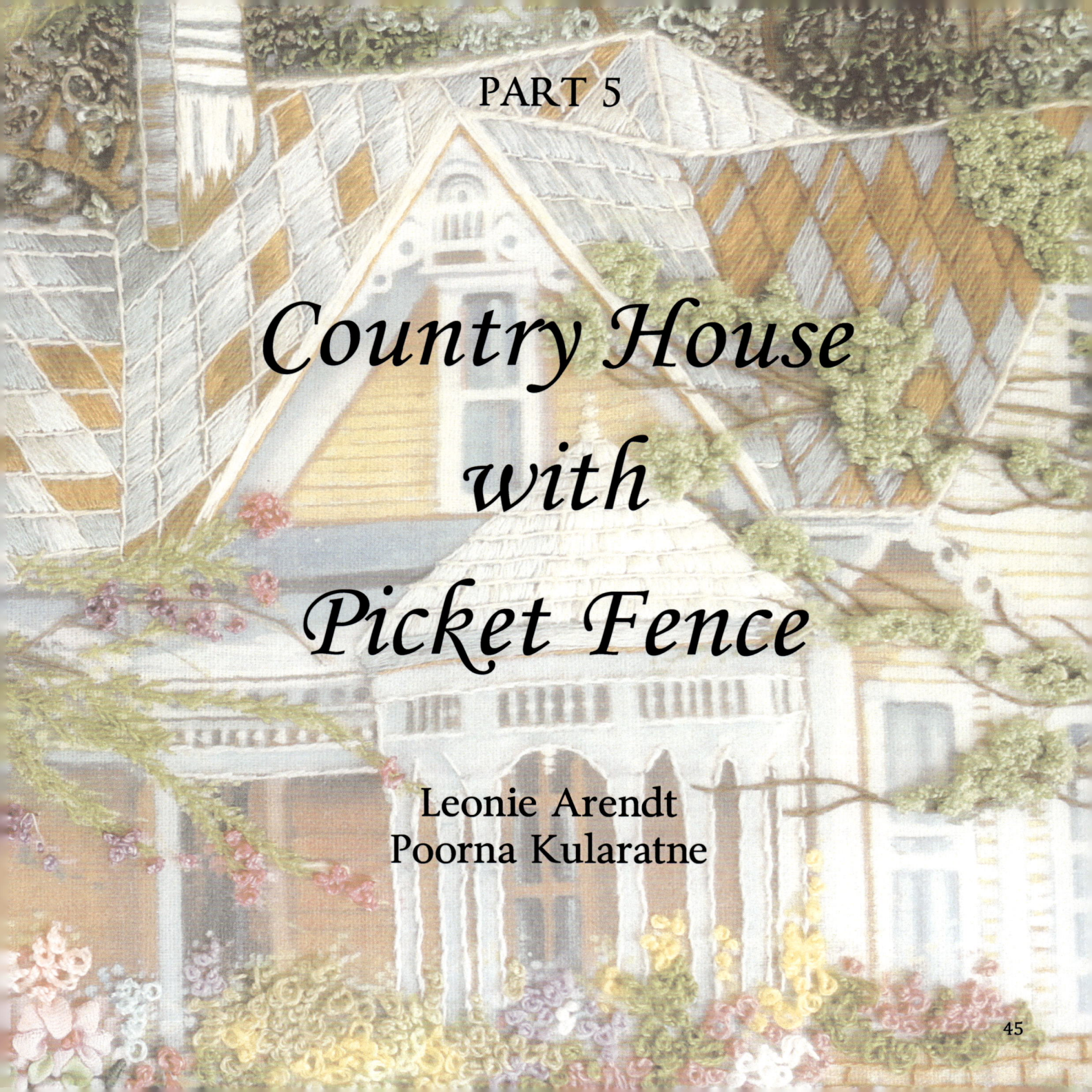

Country House with Picket Fence

Leonie Arendt
Poorna Kularatne

Leonie Arendt
Pretoria, South Africa

"In general, I love to sew in all its forms. I embroider for the past 14 years. After my retirement I moved from Pretoria to Bloemfontein. I did not know what to do with myself after a career of 35 years. One day I walked into a sewing shop and after a conversation with one of the sales ladies, I knew that I like to share this art with others. I must admit that I've learned just as hard as my embroidery friends and that's a bit more than they knew. They are my inspiration to come up with new ideas every time. I had at least sounded smarter than they do. About four years ago I returned to Pretoria and got acquainted with a group of ladies who I helped with embroidery. We enjoyed our visits and every new project is a challenge. Books give great ideas. The best is to get a picture that has very different stitching techniques and possibilities. In the garden, flowers and plants are wonderful examples and it is great joy to perfect it with ribbon.

My four children are my judges. If they 'ok' I know that's right. Fifi, my persian cat, always keep me company when I embroider. My grandsons, five of them, "birdier or knitting", as they call it, perfectly at the bottom of the picture that I am working with.

House with a Picket Fence caught my attention and I immediately saw it as a challenge. The roof has me very intrigued and I wanted the flowers, like in a real garden, hanging over the fence. Hydrangeas are always great to embroider and to make it look natural. The tree I wanted to look as natural as possible.

47

ROOF TILES
Using satin stitch, start in the middle of each tile on the roof. Fill in the left side, return to the middle and then fill in to the right. Follow the different colours alternatively until the roof is complete. The branches are worked over the roof later on.

ROOF CAMS
Outline the cams of the roof with long stem stitches from one point to another. Make as many stitches as necessary until filled line.

WINDOW AND PORCH ROOF
Outline the window with long stitches. A little mother of pearl glitter glue smeared in the windows gives it a light sheen and looks like curtains. Work four long stitches across the width of the roof. With a second needle, work short stitches spaced over these four stitches. Work four long stitches across the width of the roof. In the middle of the previous block, work a stitch over the four stitches to form a small brick. Work the bars under the roof with long stem stitches. The littles shrubs of flowers and grass are worked with French knots in colours as shown on the picture. Outline the balcony above the window with mother of pearl thread edging. Work the facia boards with long stem stitches.

FLOWERS
Work the long stem flowers with long stitches using French ribbon.

TALL SHRUB WITH PINK FLOWERS
Work the branches of the shrubs with long stem stitches. The clusters of pink flowers are done with silk ribbon using French knots. The flowers at the top are done with thread using French knots. The leaves are worked with silk ribbon using straight- and ribbon stitches.

CREEPER ON ROOF
String double thread through the needle. Work long stem stitches with green and brown French ribbon. Work a stitch on the tip of the branch with pink French ribbon to make a flower. Work the branches over the roof. See picture.

TREE BRANCH
Cut cord the length of the tree branch and as much as the thickness of the branch. Turn the cord to shape the branch. Work in place onto the fabric with small slip stitches. Split the cord threads at the bottom of the tree to resemble the roots above the ground. Split the cord at the top of the tree trunk to create the branches of the tree. Sew the separated threads in place to form the other side branches. Work the leaves with French ribbon and loose French knots.

PICKET FENCE
Work the poles of the fence with raised stem stitch. Attach strings of bouclé thread and let it hang loose over the fence. Fill the gaps with flowers.

ROSES AND OTHER FLOWERS
Group the ribbon in two different stitches: ribbon for twisted rose and thread for gathered rose. Thread sewing thread through fabric and secure. Gather through the middle of the ribbon, lengthwise. Cut ribbon and pull thread so that ribbon gathers against the fabric. Work the ends neatly away using the same thread. Follow the same method for the rest of the roses. The lilies and long blade leaves are worked with ribbon stithes.

WHITE DAISIES
Make a yellow colonial knot in the middle. Work five lazy daisy stitches around to form the flower petals. Secure the ribbon with small stitches to prevent the stitches from unravelling.

HYDRANGEAS
On a separate piece of fabric, draw a circle, 2cm in diameter and make a colonial knot. Don't pull the knot too tight. Fill the entire circle with small knots. Work small daisies here and there. Draw another circle around the first one and work small gather stitches all around. Pull the gathered thread to form a small flower ball/flower bunch. Stuff the shaped ball with a little bit of stuffing to stabilize. Fix to the background fabric with small stitches all around the ball.

LEAVES
Stretch a piece of water soluble stabilizer over an embroidery frame. Draw the amount of leaves you need onto the fabric. Work the shape of the leaf with blanket stitch. I started in the middle, fill to the left, ending at the bottom of the leaf. Start again at the top of the loop of the first stitch and work on the right side to the bottom. Cut the leaf about 2mm from the edge. Use an earbud dipped in water to gently tap around the edge of the leaf until the excess water soluble fabric disappears. Be very careful not to use too much water otherwise the stablizer inside the leaf will also dissolve and unravel the thread of the leaf. Attach the leaf carefully in between the hydrangea flowers. Outline the stone with the same colour thread as the stone. Cut a slit in the lining fabric and fill with batting and stitch closed.

POT WITH ROSES AND FRUIT SHRUB
Outline the pot. Work the roses in the pot and fill with green straight stitches for leaves. Work the creeper along the water with stab and straight stitches using silk ribbon. Attach small seed beads for the fruit. The water is gently rubbed with mother of pearl glitter glue to create a reflection on the water."

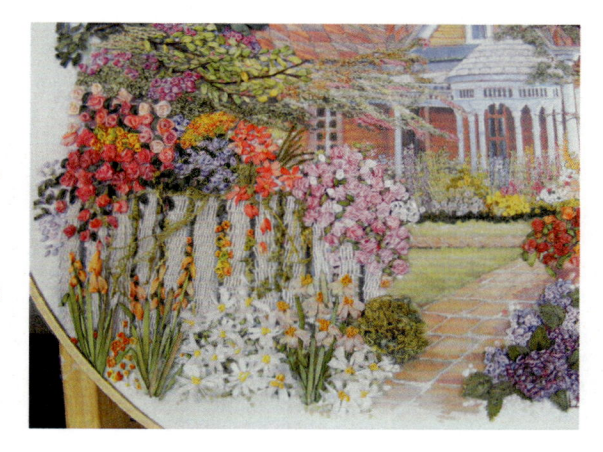

Poorna Kularatne
Mount Lavinia, Sri Lanka

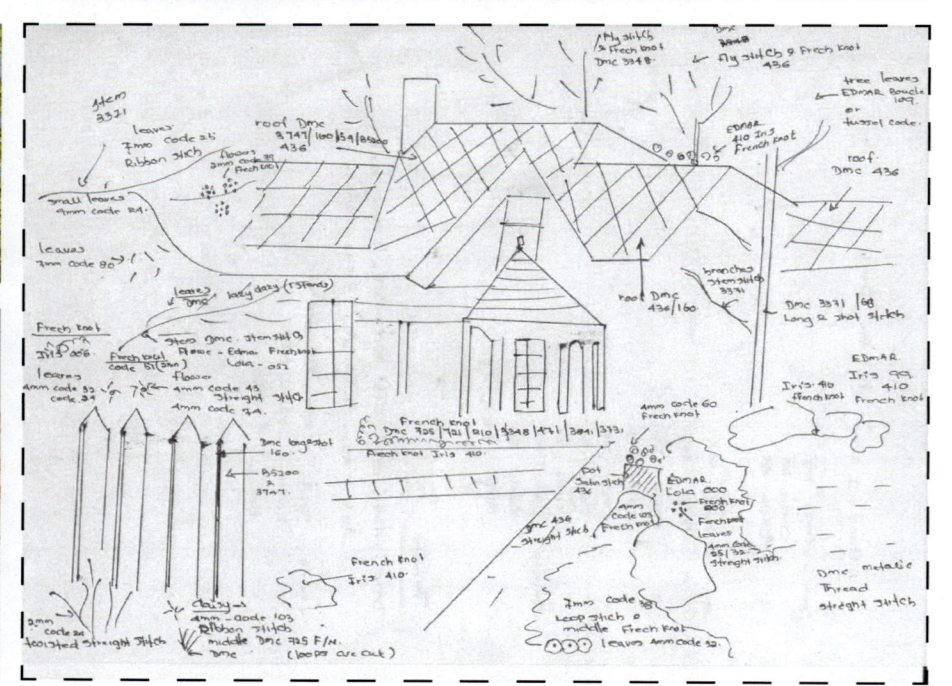

50

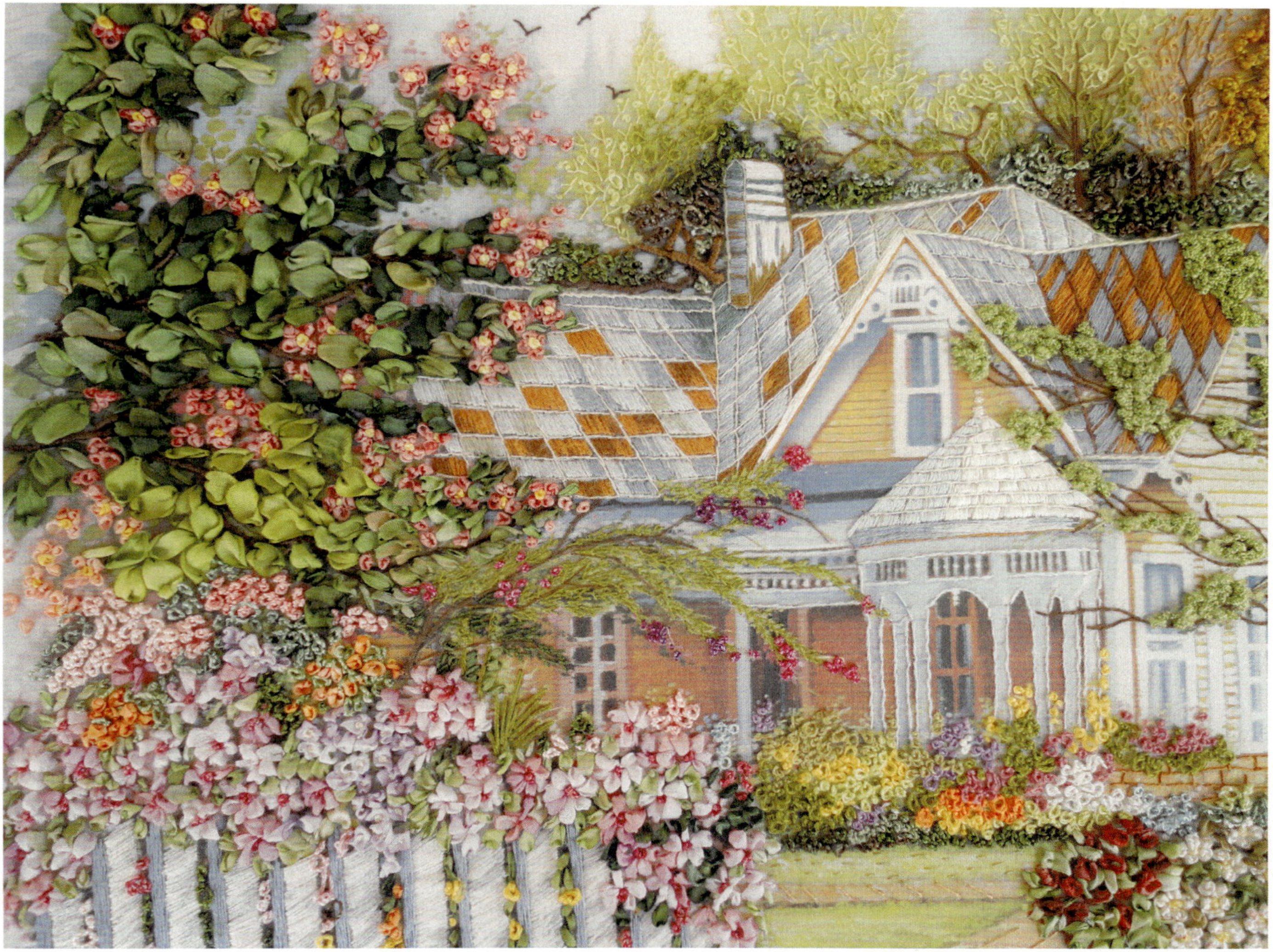

52

PART 6

Stop and Smell the Roses

Olga Smirnova

Olga Smirnova
St Petersburg, Russia

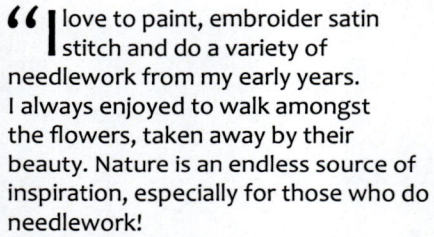

"I love to paint, embroider satin stitch and do a variety of needlework from my early years. I always enjoyed to walk amongst the flowers, taken away by their beauty. Nature is an endless source of inspiration, especially for those who do needlework!

It was my dream to find such a hobby that would become a passion, and that appeared to be ribbon embroidery!

I happened to see photos from Helen Eriksson's *Ribbon Renaissanse* on the inernet and since then I passionately wanted to learn this art.

I studied from books by Di van Niekerk, Helen Eriksson and Ann Cox; and started ribbon embroidery in January 2010.

For my projects I use various ribbons but prefer those hand dyed by Di van Niekerk! They are so, so beautiful. It's fantastic!

My *Ballerina* embroidery was awarded a special prize. I am very proud of it."

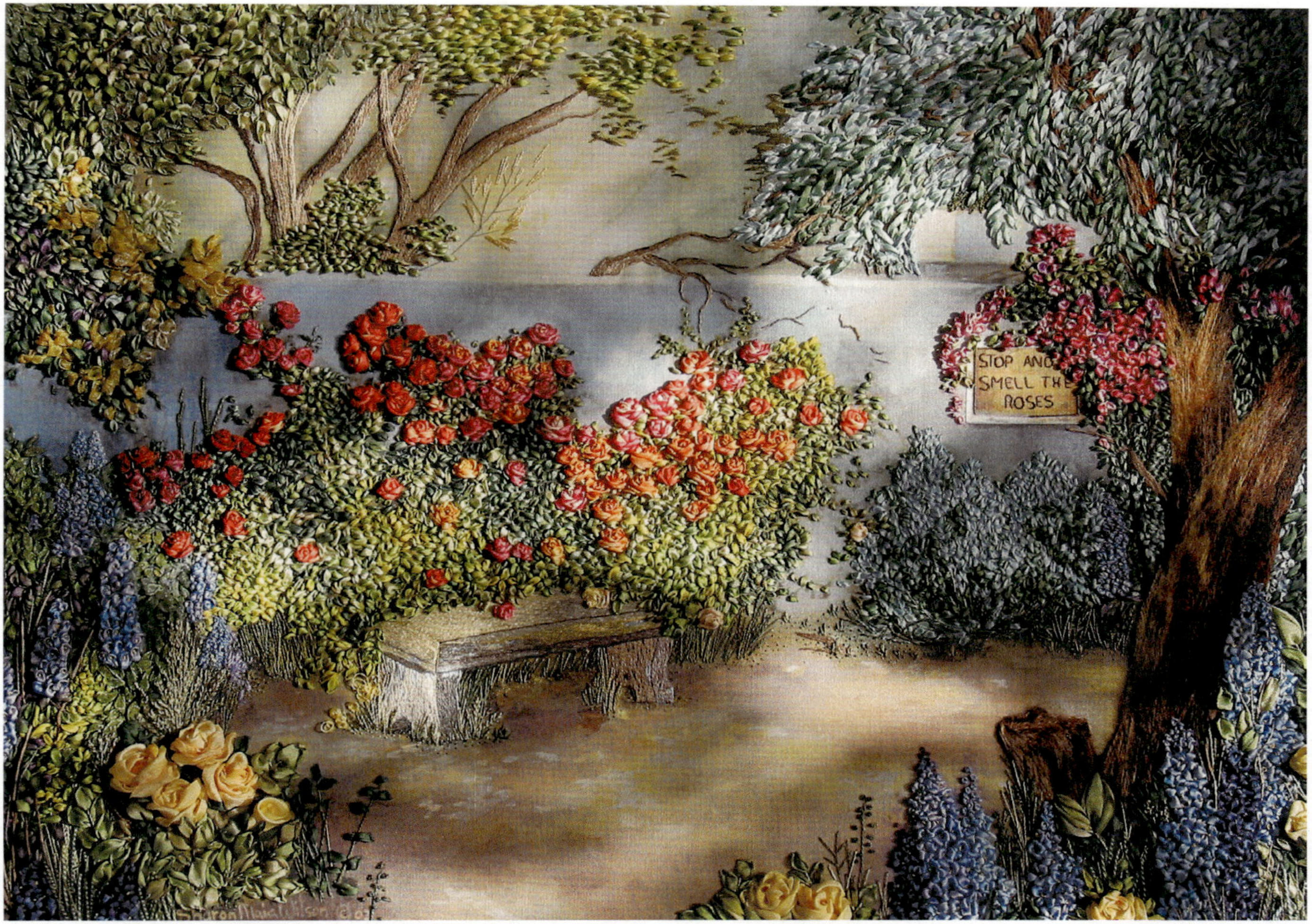
STOP AND
SMELL THE
ROSES

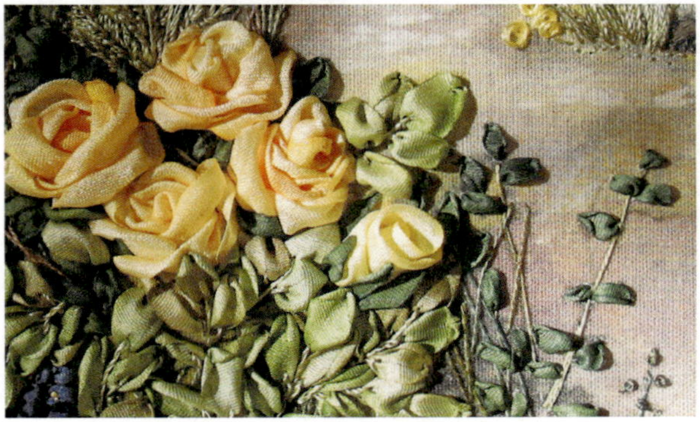

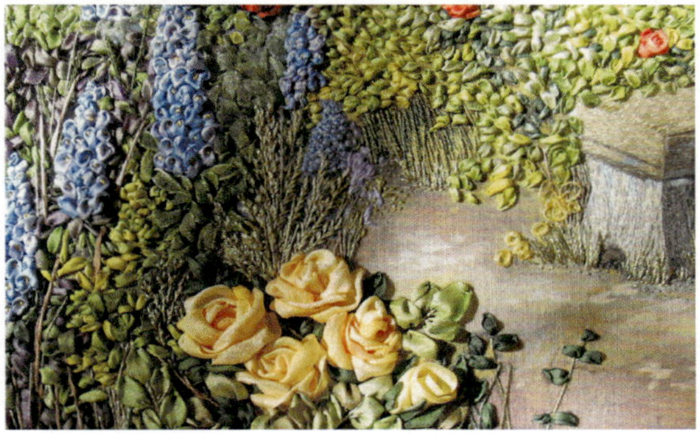

56

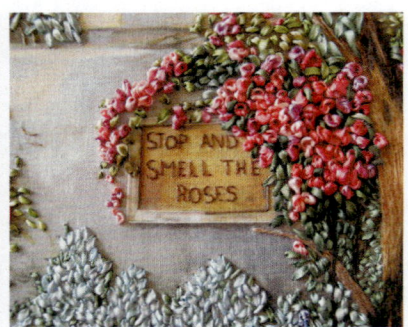

57

58

PART 7

Oranges and Bougainvillea

Larisa Torop

Larisa Torop
Psebai village, Krasnador region
Russia

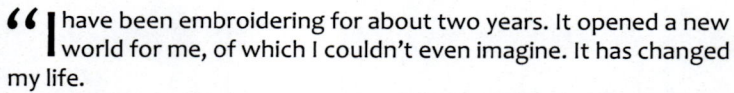

"I have been embroidering for about two years. It opened a new world for me, of which I couldn't even imagine. It has changed my life.

I embroider with ribbons and for me ribbon stitches are like the touches of a brush to the canvas. You can just draw using ribbons. Take ribbons in your hand and you can feel their streaming in your hands. They are light, flexible and gentle. The diversity of their shapes and colors gives us a lot of possiblities to create various plots, that allows to achieve incredible results, inspite of the chosen topic. We can make whatever we want using the ribbons: mighty trees, thin blades of grass, birds, butterflies and, as it seems to me, the most beautiful creation of nature: flowers.

And suddenly there is a flower just right in my hands: first of all the bud is appearing , then it starts to bloom: one petal, second, third... And then I have a bouquet, a beautiful bouquet of flowers from my garden. This is the miracle of the birth of something new. The winter is not a problem for me. My ribbons help me to feel a breath of fresh spring wind. They can make my dreams come true.

It is incredible joy for me. When I create something I have a lot of new ideas, and I am always in a hurry to implement them in my work. There are no two absolutely identical flowers in nature, and neither in the ribbons. Every stitch is unique. It has its own curve, magic and beauty.

I put a piece of my soul in my work and I believe that it will certainly warm the soul of another person, who will have my embroidery or maybe someone will just give a glance at it , but his soul will be warmed either, and this fact makes me happy.

"I used beads to create oranges in my embroidery and give a relief effect.

I sanded the beads and then I covered them with silk thread. You can see a tree made of wool and mohair thread in the background. It looks like it has been painted by aquarelle pencils.

I stuck some pieces of raw amber on the flowerbed. I used green wool on the top of amber to give it volume.

I embroidered little flowers in a thin green silk ribbon. One end of the ribbon I streched through the wool at the base of the picture; the other one is freely hanging over the amber making its own shadow."

62

63

64

PART 8

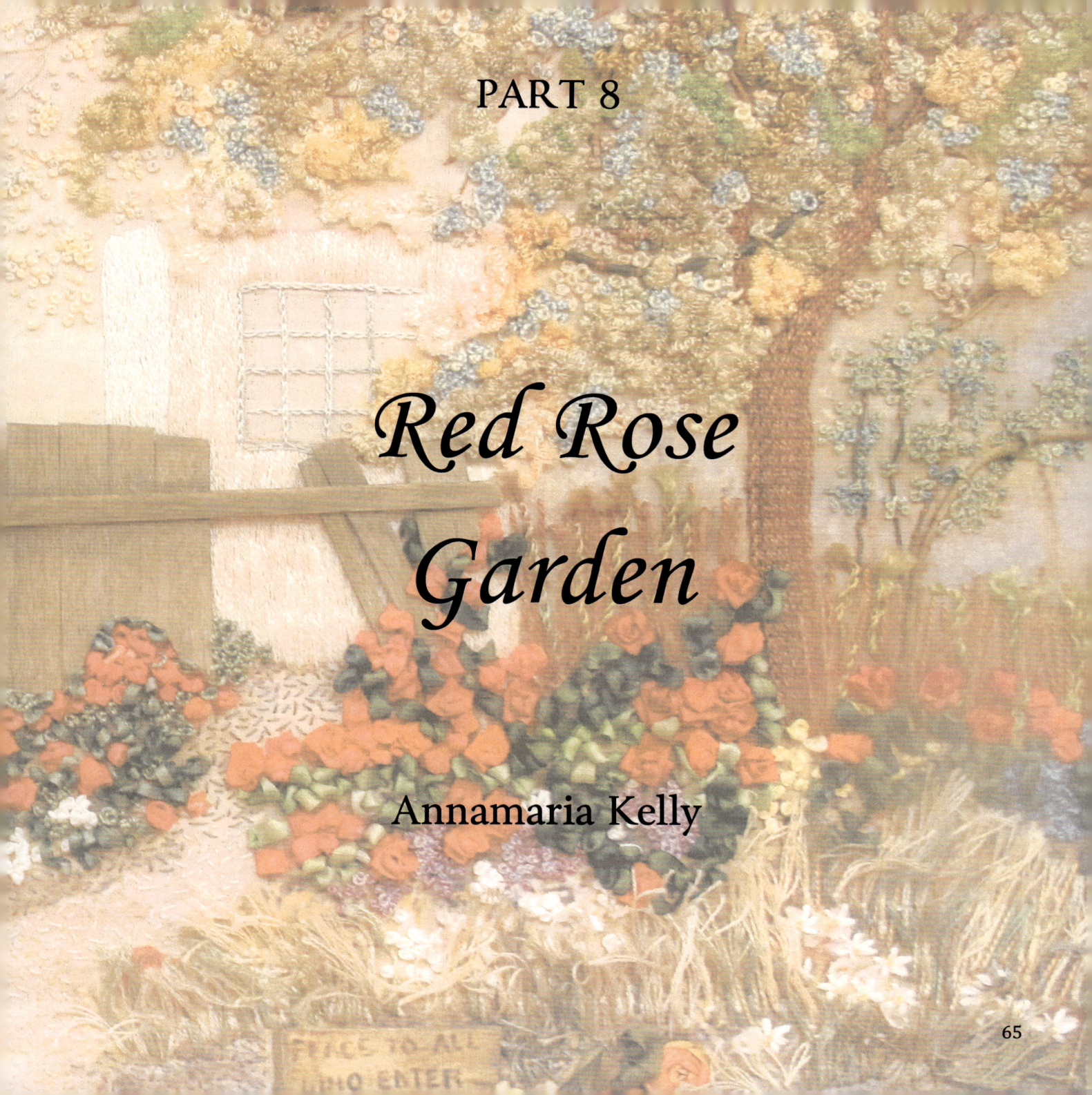

Red Rose Garden

Annamaria Kelly

Annamaria Kelly
Fourways, Johannesburg
South Africa

"My passion for embroidery was sparked when I walked into Di Van Niekerk's shop in 2002. The shop was beautifully laid out with lovely embroidered items, quilts and furniture. Di approached me to ask if I would like to embroider and I remember laughing because although I can sew, embroidery was not on my radar. I did not even know how to do a chain stitch but I learn fast and once I understood the concept there was no stopping me. I was hooked from day one. I am passionate about different types of embroidery, my two favourites being ribbon and the other crewel.

I work as a Principal Engineering Administrator for an engineering company during the week and teach a full class of ladies every alternate Saturday afternoon. I get immense pleasure teaching my students. My oldest student is 90 years old and my youngest was 14 years old.

I have two daughters, one lives in Australia and the other lives near me. I share my home with my partner and five Yorkshire Terriers.

I wanted to do something different and chose one of the pictures that I didn't think many people would do. The fence was made with balsa wood which was fine tuned many times to fit in with a much loved garden. I try to break the rules and think out of the box. I am passionate about being creative and different.

I am basically a free style embroiderer and I break the rules all the time. Rules are meant to be broken when you are being creative. A trick of mine is to walk away from my picture, and in fact I leave the room. Then I walk back in again focussing on my picture and if something is wrong or looks wrong, you will see it immediately.

Most important of all, enjoy what you are doing. There is no right way or wrong way. I like using different textures but if you are happy to only use thread and ribbon, the choice is entirely yours.

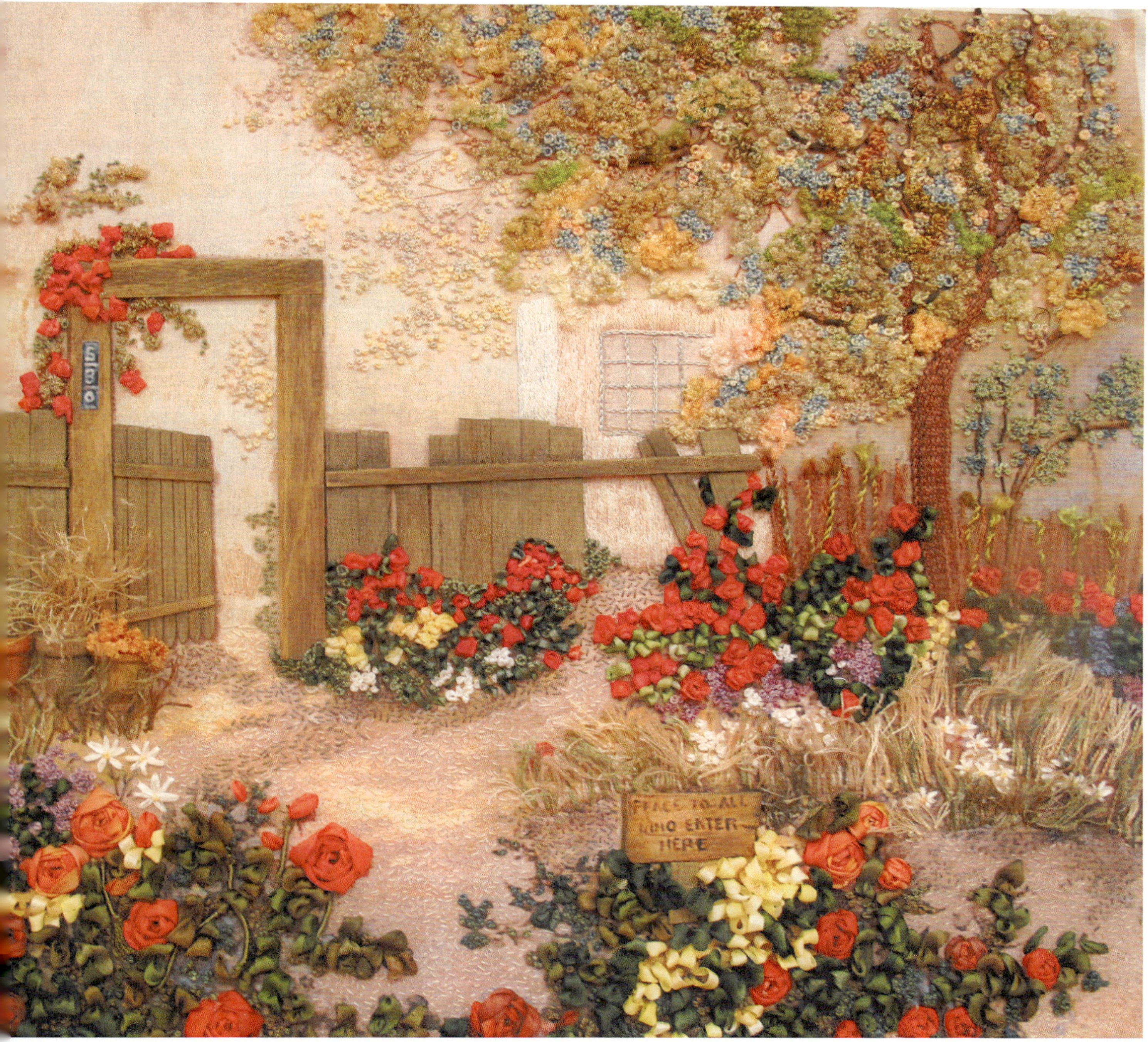
PEACE TO ALL
WHO ENTER
HERE

LITTLE POTS

Paint three little pots in the colour of your choice then stick to picture. Add soft bouclé yarn to give a soft effect to the picture. I am fond of using fluffy wool in order to get a good effect. Foliage in the middle of picture – left and right of picture. Here I have used a combination of long strands of thread using single loop stitches. Keep making stitches on top of each other then cut the loop so that the grass falls in different directions. Add fluffy strands of wool as well. Mess it up a bit to make it look a little untidy. After all it is a garden. Once the grass looks good, add small French knots here and there in purple and white threads.

FOLIAGE

Again, make French knots all over then fill in with bouclé wools in soft colours like green, pink and silver. Fill in with ribbon stitches.

ROSES

Using silk ribbon make colonial knots running stitch roses where the roses are on the picture. Use different colour reds to get a lovely soft effect. Add yellow roses making French knots using silk ribbon.

ROSE GARDEN

With silk ribbon make soft spider web roses. Fill in bushes with French knots in cotton perlé and ribbon stitches. Add some white daisies.

CACTUS

Draw on a piece of green felt separate pieces of the cactus then long and short stitch these. Apply anti-fray agent and wait until dry then cut out. Starting from the back, attach the cactus to the picture.

HOUSE
Outline the window with very small chain stitches using one strand grey thread. With the colour of your choice, long and short stitch the house. Outline the corner in a different colour to give dimension to the picture.

TREE FOLIAGE
Using a variety of soft green, pink, yellow and cream cotton perlé stranded threads and work French knots all over. Fill in with a variety of pink, soft green, beige bouclé yarns.

TREE
Outline branches with thin covered wire or dried twigs. You can also stem stitch the branches with brown cotton perlé thread.

At the bottom right hand corner and middle of the picture I worked seed stiches to cover the ground with the various shades of thread. Work horizontal stitches along the tree trunk with cotton perlé thread. Work in raised stem stitch on top of horizontal stitches in the same colour. Couch on thin pieces of covered wire or wood in place for the branches.

WOODEN FENCE
A good friend made the wooden fence for me out of balsa wood but one can easily embroider the fence. If you want to add bulk to the fence, you can use felt and then sew on top. If using wood, stick the fence to the picture. Once the fence was attached and dry, I made small little French knot roses which I cut then stuck with a little glue to the fence frame. Keep going until you get the look you are happy with. Add in some soft pieces of bouclé yarn around the frame. Be careful if you are working with the balsa wood as it can crack and break easily. Either embroider the sign or make one."

70

PART 9

Fleur gathering flowers with Manon

Oya Altinkök

"I learned the art of patchwork in 2008 and embroidery in 2009. My aquaintance with patchwork and embroidery has directed my life in a positive way. Every design and step as I embroider makes me happy and gives me pleasure. This is my greatest indulgence. Patchwork and embroidery gives me peace. Every design I embroider and every colour I add to my artwork opens new vistas. When I handle my threads and ribbons I feel happy watching them.

The secret is to love this art. When I start the rest glides on its own. When you add your effort and soul to your love these beautiful designs are created. The inspiration comes from God. Everything develops on its own. A little photograph, an object from nature, a magazine gives me different ideas, as if a flash of lightening. I add original detail to my artwork with different applications.

A lot of effort and patience is required. It takes a lot of my time, but people who see the result can feel my emotions. Appreciation of my work makes me happy and encourages me to do better and different designs.

I received an award in the 2008 ANCHOR competition. I received an award in the competition arranged by the Bursa Governorship and Uluumay Museum. I staged an exhibiton in Germany as the Governorship's artist.

I exhibited my artwork at the Bursa 1st International Arab Fair. I participated in a patchwork exhibiton in Izmir Alacati. These awards I have achieved motivate and commit me to my work."

Oya Altinkök
Nilüfer/Bursa, Turkey

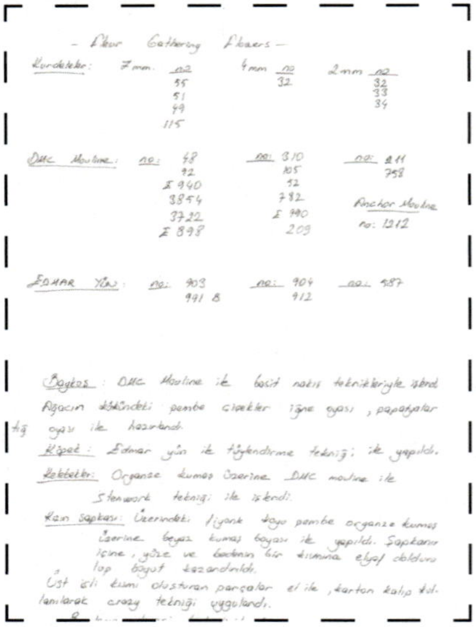

73

The flowers were embroidered with ribbon and stranded cotton. The hat and gloves were crocheted with no 5 cotton perlé. The flowers were embroidered with ribbon and filled with fiber and sewn. The couch was embroidered with mouline and shaped with woven fabric and coloured with textile dyes. After embroidering was completed the artwork was framed with gobelin fabric with DMC design. A curtain was mounted with lace and taffeta fabrics. The cat in front of the window was applied with applique technique with velvet and dimension was given with textile dyes. A curtain design was created this way.

75

76

PART 10

Danielle cuddling her Baby Chick

Elena Lisovitskaya

Elena Lisovitskaya
Lugansk, Ukraine

Lugansk is not a big city with the population about 300 000 people. I am a lawyer by profession and work according to my speciality. I am fond of drawing since my childhood, and have always been interested in various kinds of handcraft. A few years ago I happened to see the picture in a magazine, which was ribbon embroidery, and I just could not hold myself and couldn't pass by. I bought the magazine and wanted to make something like that, but at that same time did not dare to do it because I thought it was too difficult. Last year I was amazingly attracted by very beautiful ribbon embroidered pictures which I saw on the internet and this time I've decided to open up and learn this kind of embroidery. I have been studying by the books and the internet. When I started to deal with embroidery, I began to look differently at the world, and to perceive notions in a different way. I began to notice the things which I previously did not pay much attention to: small blades of grass, dews, delicate colour of flower petals, graceful curves of stems. The world began to seem more kind and more beautiful to me.

    Ribbon embroidery makes me constantly think, perceive, invent new methods for realization of my imagination and it is perfectly combined with other techniques. My five year old son Alexander chose the picture of *Danielle cuddling her baby chick*. He liked the girl with the chickens and asked me to embroider it. In this handcraft also several techniques are used: embroidery, braiding, knitting, felting and appliqué.

SWEATER
I used embroidery thread to knit the sweater using tapestry needles with blunt ends instead of knitting needles. The blunt ends prevent the loops from slipping down. I used a comparatively short thread which connects the needles' eyes. At first knit the collar and fix to the fabric. Then weave the sweater body and attach the bottom 'band'. The sleeve is weaved as a separate unit and is attached to the fabric using the design as a guide. When attaching the sleeve, first fix three sides, then attach a patch on the elbow beneath the sleeve. Insert a bit of stuffing to give volume, and then fix the fourth side of the sleeve.

HAT
I used knitting yarn for the hat. The top is weaved as a basket. The hat brim is sewn to the fabric base; and lifted and shaped over the side of the face. The ribbon is attached to the base along the short sides. A bow is fixed on top.

HAIR
Locks of doll's hair are inserted though a needle and sewed the same way as thread, but the ends are left loose. To make a braid take long strands and plait a braid. Tie a ribbon bow around the loose ends and attach to the fabric with small stitches.

JEANS
Work the seams with fine stitches using a thin dark sewing thread.

CHICKS
The chicks are made with yellow felt and felting yarn; black sewing thread for the eyes; orange sewing thread for the beaks and feet. Outline the chicken shape on felt. Roll a small piece of yellow felting wool up into a ball. Attach it to felt with a felting needle, creating the desired shape. Felt, which makes the background, should be left uncoated. These are chicken wings and tails. To make bulge wings and tails attach small pieces of felt with a special felting needle. Fix the chicken on the design and add some brown color with a watercolour pencil.

GRASS AND FLOWERS
Use green and brown stranded cotton to work the grass and stones. The flowers are worked with silk ribbon.

80

PART 11

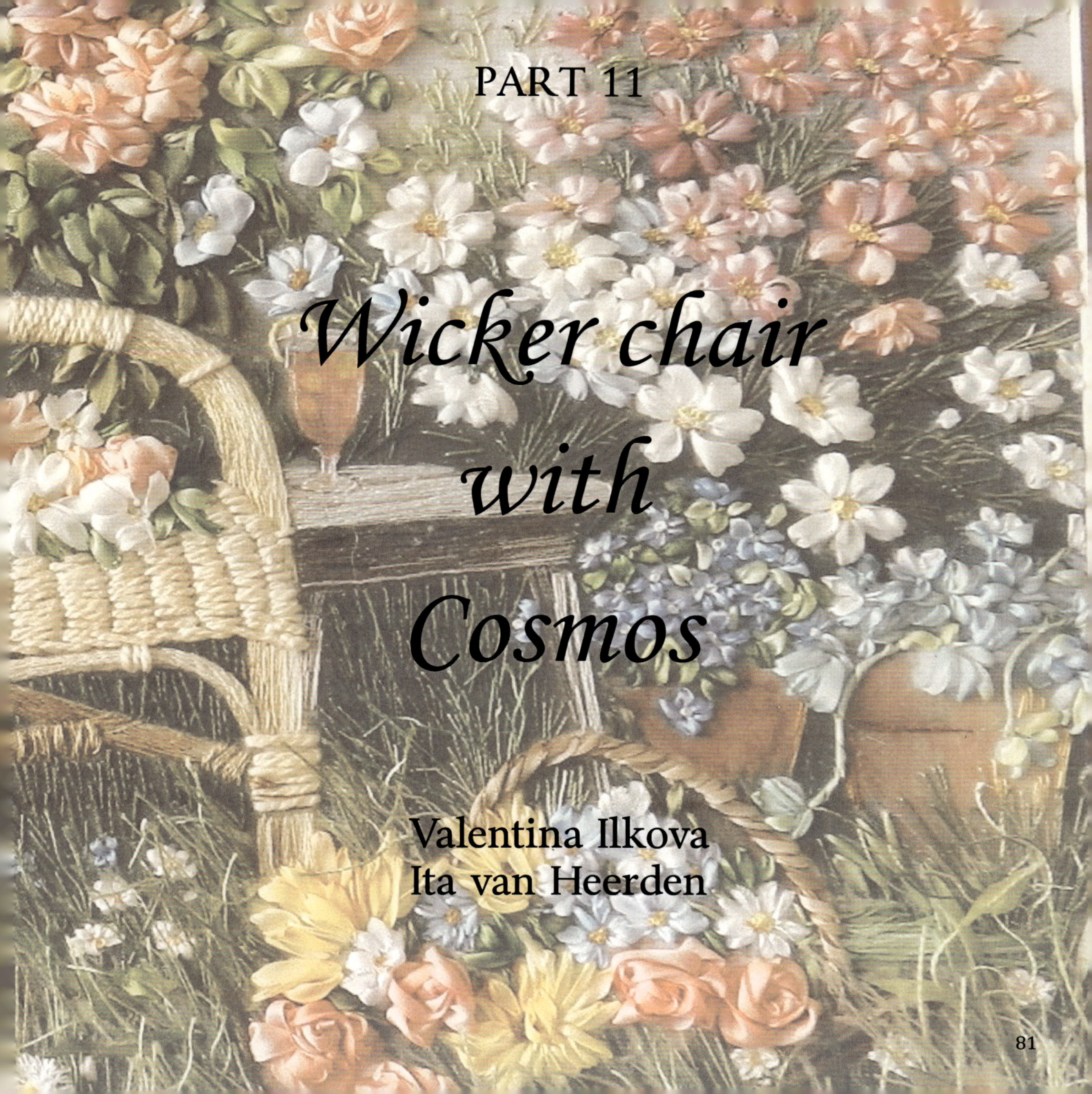

Wicker chair with Cosmos

Valentina Ilkova
Ita van Heerden

Valentina Ilkova
Nakhodka, Primorsky Krai
Russia

"My first introduction to ribbon embroidery was in 2006, having bought a book by E Cox, *Embroidery Silk Ribbons*. In our little town nobody embroiders with ribbons and I have tried to learn from the book itself. I got it and it gave me confidence in my abilities. I began to search for other books to develop my imagination and learn new techniques of embroidery ribbons. My reference books are E Erikson, J Gibb and Di van Niekerk. It is a great joy to be the owner of these wonderful books.

The inspiration for me is not only to re-create their excellent work, but this is an example of excellence, like the flowers and scenes in which they are depicted. As a child I drew a lot, but eventually drawing skills got lost; but the ribbons captured me that everything else faded into the background. I love to sew and always find time for my favourite hobbies. I chose this project because I liked the picture. I wanted to test my abilities and how to show the volumetric details on print, embroider the chair and hat so that they looked like the real thing. Embroidered ribbon flowers, the roses behind the chair look so real and the ribbon shows the tenderness of the cosmos. I use all the different ribbon widths to also try to embroider little flowers so that they are still visible. In this project, you can make a lot of three-dimensional parts, which I tried to show."

"I did different stitches with silk ribbon such as ribbon, straight, folded and twisted stitches as well as French knots. I used different stitches together like on the straw hat.
For the smoother surfaces I used embroidery threads where I applied straight stitches. I also worked French knots with thread for the flower centres.
Special techniques, such as trapunto, were used to give volume to some areas like the hat, arms of the chair and flower pots.
Some small flowers were done separately with Turkey stitches using thread. After the loops were cut the base of the small flowers were fixed to the long grass in the foreground.
The arms of the chair are made with trapunto and embroidered with satin stitch.
The hat is embroidered with chain stitches worked very dense and close together. I wanted to create a woven effect. A different shade thread was used to create the bit of shading on the one side.
The long grass was made with Turkey stitches. After cutting the thread, the long blades cut from the leaves and ribbon glued on top of the long grass. Lightly fluff the cut threads to give it a natural look.
The stems of the bouquet on the chair are wire wrapped with thread. The bouquet is then glued to the the background.
The glass on the table is covered with transparent gel to make it look like real glass."

83

84

85

Ita van Heerden
Pretoria, Gauteng
South Africa

"I was born in 1933 in Ceres in the Western Cape Province, where I also went to school. I married a soldier in 1958 and we were stationed through the Republic of South Africa as well as in Kazakhstan. I have three sons and four grandchildren. I live in Pretoria. After my husband passed away in 2009, I kept myself busy with embroidery and other needlework. I attend a group of ladies who embroider once a week. Since I've started embroidery I've finished 43 pictures. I love to embroider landscapes and flowers. Nature is my biggest inspiration.

Thank you for the opportunity to take part in this book. I would also like to thank my embroidery friends and teachers for their support and inspiration."

"The chair is worked with raised stem stitches.

The sides are worked in the same manner, but vertically. I used cord for the arm rests and stitched it to the background with small stitches.

The flowers on the chair are done with ribbon stitches with French knots as the flower centres using yellow thread.

The stems are worked with long stitches.

The gloves are done with long and short stitch.

I worked the daisies with white rayon thread and leaves between the flowers with stranded cotton.

The petals of the Hibiscus flowers, daisies and cosmos are worked with ribbon stitches and French knots in the centres. The leaves are done in ribbon stitch.

For the basket I used spider stitch.

I crocheted the hat, starting with three chain stitches and worked a small circle. Increase by one stitch in each chain stitch. Continue to increase for six to eight rows. Now continue for another eight rows without increasing, until it looks like a thimble. Work a long leg in each of the previous row of stitches. Make two long legs in the first stitch. Work six long legs. Then work two long legs in the next stitch. Repeat until the edge is long enough. Stuff the hat ball with a small piece of batting. Carefully attach the hat to the chair with small stitches. Wrap a piece of ribbon around the ball and work small roses on the ribbon to finish off.

For the Delphinium stems, work straight stitches from top to bottom. For the flowers work small daisy-like stitches on and around the stems."

87

88

PART 12

Rose sampler

Kristina Nilsson
Mania Badmagrian

Kristina Nilsson
Piteå, Sweden

"I have always done things with my hands – knitting, crochet, lacemaking and clothes for myself and my children – but I never liked embroidery!

In 2004 my husband and I moved to Tanzania for one year. We fell in love with Africa already in 1986 when we worked in Maputo, Moçambique.

In Dar es Salaam, Tanzania, I met a South African lady, Michelle Lilly, who inspired me to try creative ribbon embroidery, then unknown to me. I was sold after the first class! This was something much more creative than the embroidery I practiced before. When I got back to Sweden, I wanted everybody to try it and discover this fantastic art.

I forced almost all my friends and relatives to try it out.

My problem was to get this wonderful silk ribbon that I used in Tanzania. It was impossible to find in Sweden and I tried many ribbons but I was never satisfied. Until I started to import materials from South Africa. I started a business, Creative Embroidery of Sweden, and give classes. Now I'm out on different fairs in Sweden to show and inspire others to try embroidery and I teach on a regular basis, all year round.

My interest in nature and gardening gives me the ideas and inspiration for my embroidery. And of course, all my students give me different challenges so solve!

I live on a small island near the Arctic Circle in Piteå, Sweden. This is me in my garden during winter when, up here in the north, the snow is more than one meter thick; it is cold and just a few hours daylight. During the long dark winters there is plenty of opportunities to do what I like most: creative embroidery."

"I mainly did my picture by reading the instructions in Di´s book *Roses in silk and organza ribbon*. It wasn't always easy, and sometimes I had to make the rose twice and even three times to get it as I wanted. Occasionally I made the leaves and butterflies in another technique than described in the book.

I embroidered the Fig Tree Blue butterfly with raw silk thread."

91

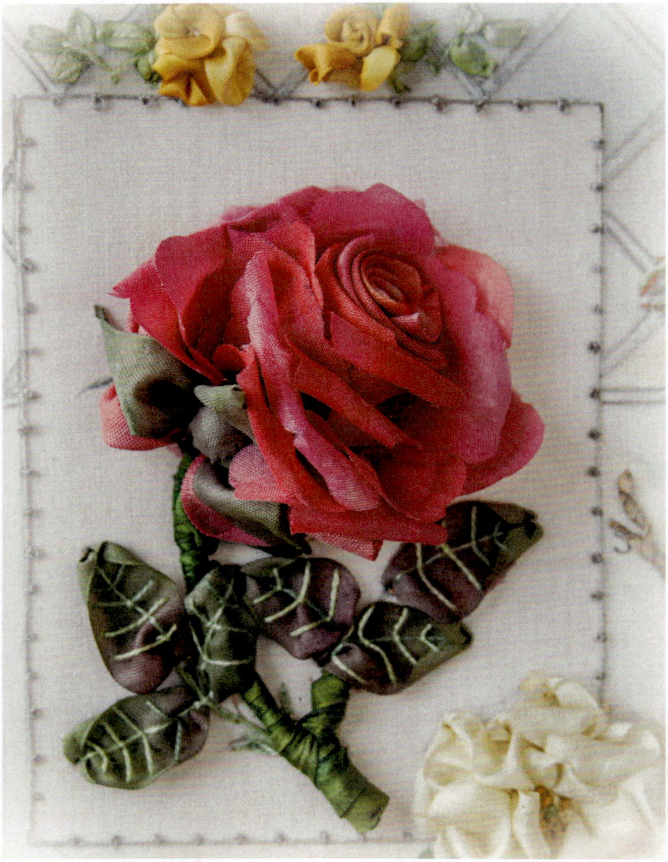

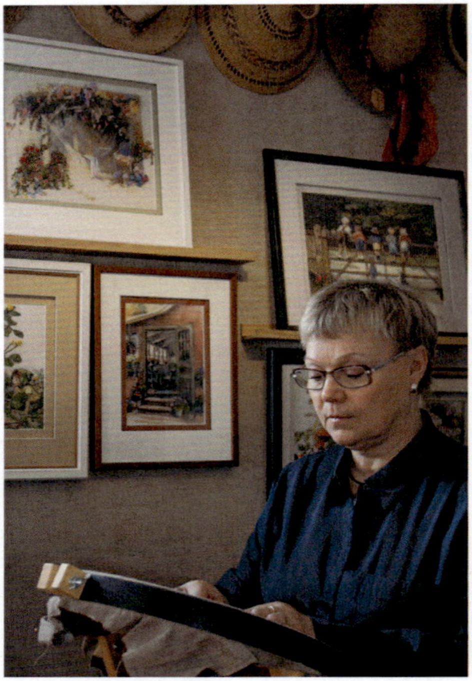

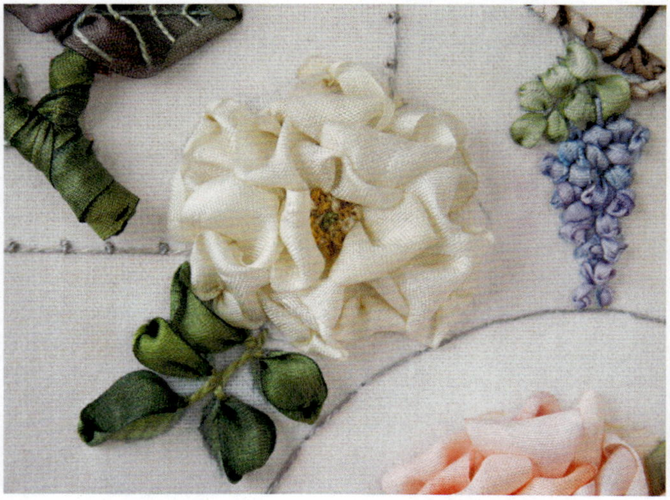

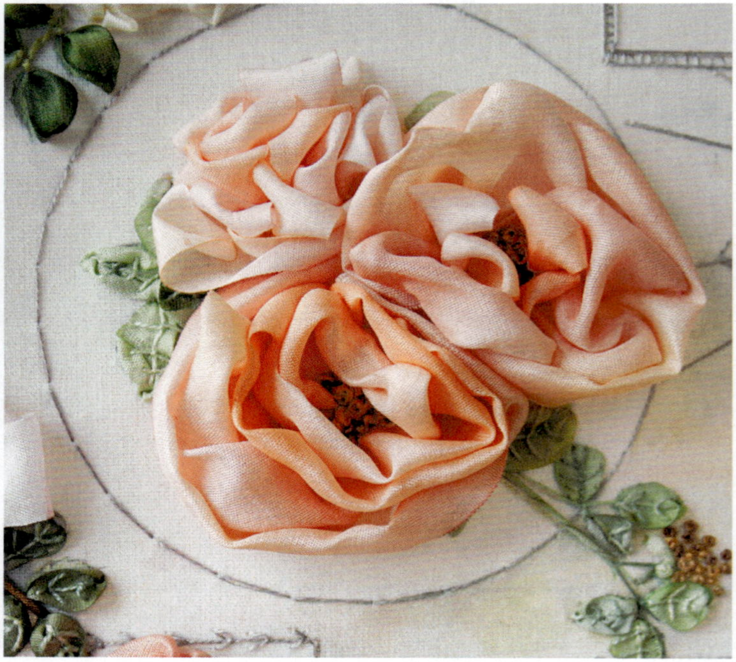

93

94

95

Mania Badmagrian
Glendale, California
United States of America

"I was born and raised in Iran. I did my first embroidery when I was 12 years old under the supervision of my aunt who was an excellent stitcher.

I am residing in the United States since 1985. A few years ago I saw Di van Niekerk's *Ribbon Embroidery & Stumpwork* book and ordered it along with the design fabric panel. I finished the embroidery and took it to 2007 Brazilian Embroidery Show at Portland Oregon where I recevied an award for my work. I got another of Di's books and panels, *A Perfect World in Ribbon Embroidery & Stumpwork*. I also did three projects from Di's book *Dreamscapes*.

In 2010 my students and friends gave me Di's *Roses in silk and organza* book together with the sampler panel and some ribbons as a 'get well' gift. I could hardly wait to get well enough to be able to start that lovely project. It took me a year to finish it and I enjoyed every one of those different roses.

Embroidery is my hobby, my best friend and my therapy. I am very thankful to Di van Niekerk for her artful designs and renovated techniques."

97

98

PART 13

Girl reaching

Jane Stilgoe
Carol Bianconi
Claire Rubie

Jane Stilgoe
Booleroo Centre
South Australia

"I was born in former Rhodesia, now Zimbabwe, in 1955 and started embroidering whilst at nursing school at Bulawayo Central Hospital in 1975.

Embroidery became a lot more important to me in the late 90's when a very talented lady attempted to teach some friends and I how to do ribbon embroidery. The others took to the art like ducks to water but I was decidedly the worst of the bunch. But I was hooked and have persevered and loved ribbon embroidery since that time.

For me it is the most thrilling craft. Each new project offers new opportunities to try different things. I loved mixing the stump work with traditional ribbon and exploring craft shops for new materials eg the hemp twine to provide texture and interest. For me, embroidery is a fitting and wonderful end to a busy day when I can curl up on the couch with a cup of tea and reach for my stitching. I treasure these hours and am so grateful to be able to totally relax doing something I love."

HAIR
"Take thread from the front with tail left at length desired. Work a tiny straight stitch. Bring thread again from the back to the front and cut to desired length. Continue along hair line until filled. Second hair line starts lower down but under the first to fill the head. Short hairs around face done in the same way and cut to desired length and glued in place.

JEANS
The belt is made of a 4mm-strip brown felt stitched in place with tiny stab stitches at both ends and edged in tiny cross stitches in matching thread. Loops on the belt are stitched with matching embroidery thread – three straight stitches woven. Loops stand away from fabric so that belt could be threaded through. The label is done in satin stitch with metallic gold thread, single strand. The heart is outlined with metallic turquoise thread, single strand.

GIRL
The body was stitched in parts beginning with the arm and hand, then the cheek, jersey and finally the jeans. Backing fabric pinned in place and back-stitched around each part with invisible thread. A small slit cut in the backing fabric and each part stuffed with fibre filling for toys using a toothpick and small tweezers. Overstitch to complete.

101

TREES

For the branches I used natural hemp cord, couched with stranded cotton, then whipped with crewel wool. The shaded trees on the far right, in the distance, were backstitched. The smaller trees are worked in natural hemp couched with matching thread. The upper leaves are worked with detached chain stitches, single thread. The lower yellow leaves are worked with double twist colonial knots."

LEAVES

"For variation in colour and to provide texture I mixed my leaves doing some in stumpwork and some in ribbon stitch. I made the stumpwork leaves by fixing 38mm-wide organza ribbon onto firm organza fabric with embroidery adhesive and stretched this onto a hoop. I drew the leaves and stitched them, alternating fishbone, open fishbone stitch and split stitched edges and veins. Some leaves were loosely ribbon stitched with 4mm organza ribbon matching the central vein with a single strand thread."

VINE

"I drew 42 leaves onto 38mm organza ribbon, fixed to organza fabric as before and stretched over a hoop. I split stitched along the edges and central vein, in a matching single stranded thread. I cut out the leaves and dabbed the edges with anti-fray solution. I made 14 dark leaves with stumpwork using fishbone stitches. There are 23 sun-bleached leaves on which I loosely ribbon stitched in organza ribbon. The central vein is done in straight stitch with a single strand. The vine stems are backstitched with cotton perlé thread, then whipped with silk ribbon."

PATH AND STONES

"Work seed stitches in the path, single strand. The stones are stumpworked from a second embroidery panel, stuffed with fibre filling and secured with tiny stab stitches. Grasses on path are done with straight stitches using silk ribbon. "

FLOWERS

"The flowers were done with bullion knots, ribbon stitch and woven spider's web stitch. Tiny flowers are worked in chain stitch."

GRASSES

"The grasses are done with stem stitch and the flax with twisted ribbon stitch secured with tiny stab stitches in matching thread. The bullrush leaves are worked in straight stitches couched with matching thread. The bullrush heads are done with looped bullions.

BIRD'S NEST
I sculpted the bird's nest with natural and handpainted raffia working loose straight stitches. I then fixed real soft chick feathers in the base with fabric glue. The eggs are stumpworked in white felt cut to size and satin stitched in white rayon thread, single strand.

SHOES
The shoes are stumpworked in dark brown felt and secured in place with tiny stab stitches in matching thread, single strand."

Carol Bianconi
Huntington Beach, California
United States of America

"I have been stitching hardanger and silk ribbon for the past seven years. The first project I did was the *Red Clover Flower Fairy* which I entered into a judged Embroidery Guild of America Show in Palos Verdes, California. The piece received a third place. The *Maiden with the Horse* received a second place ribbon. This will be submitted in their 2014 Show. When I first saw Di's *Flower Fairy* book, I was hooked! I took several classes from Karen Fraser at Piecemakers in Costa Mesa, California learning techniques and stitches. I finally felt confident to tackle the Red Clover Flower Fairy, my first endeavor in silk ribbon embroidery. I have since completed many other projects from Di either from her books or web site. I am still trying to perfect the Roses! I have become fairly proficient in Hardanger Embroidery and have taught beginning classes at Piecemakers."

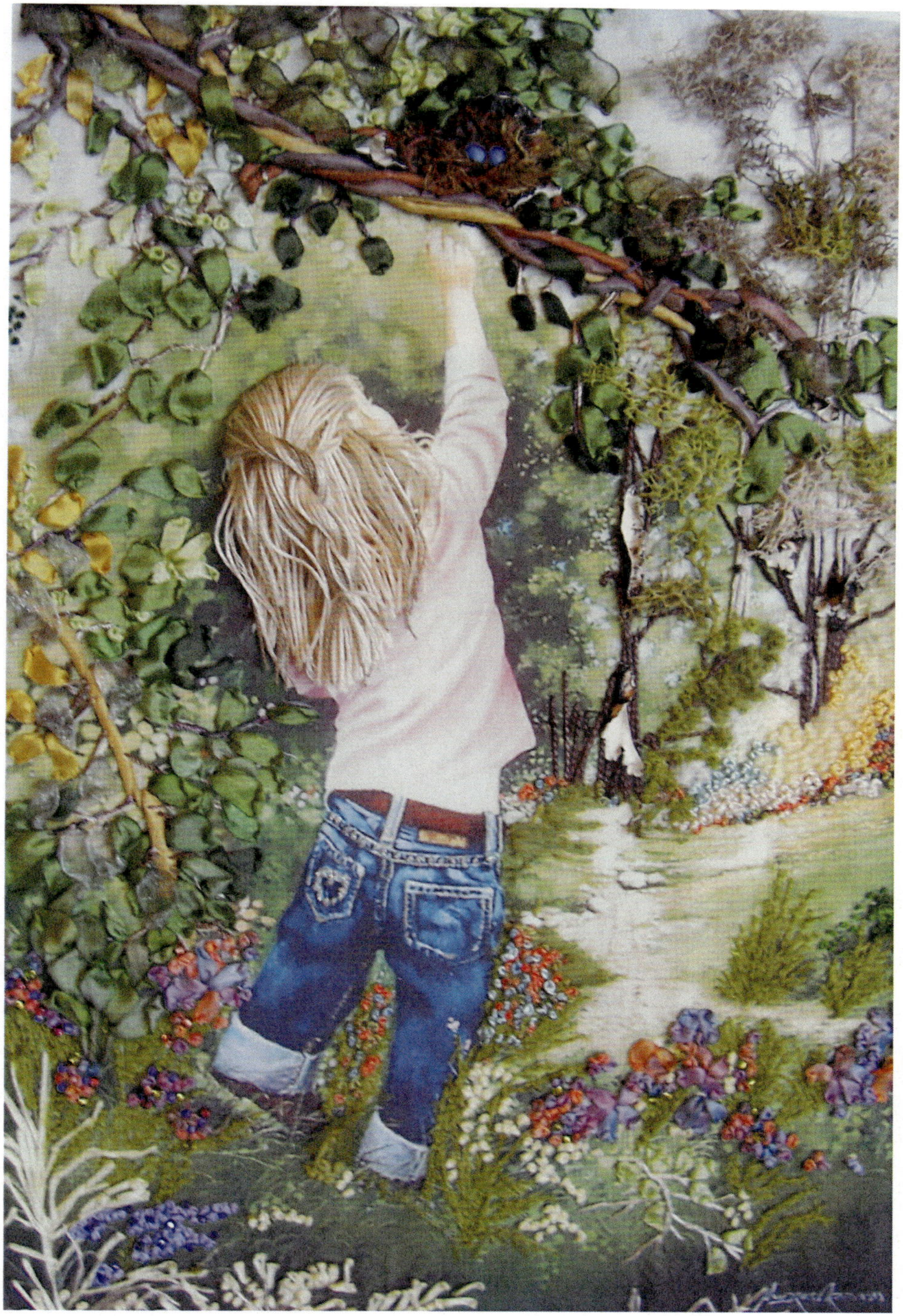

"The hair was done in a combination of two colors – light tan and light brown.

The individual strands were knotted from the back and pulled through leaving about a 6-inch tail. I continued to cover the head with the individual strands, then braided the center and sides to the back and tied it off. The hair was then shaped using hair spray until I had what I was looking for. Then trimmed to the desired length.

Any time I have done this method of hair it is important to leave long tails until you are ready to cut and shape.

The background trees were done with sea sponge and real wood bark and glued in place.

The main tree branch used three colours of satin cord, twisted and tacked down with floss.

The flowers in the fields were French knots using overdyed floss.

I used various beads for accent colour in the flowers and the heart on her jeans."

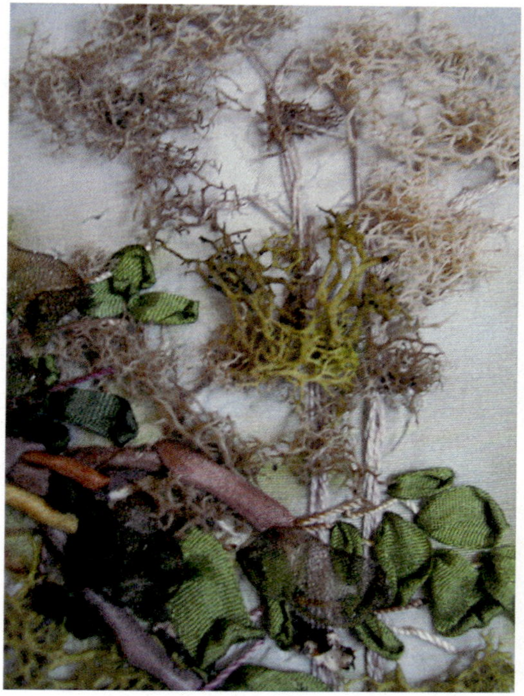

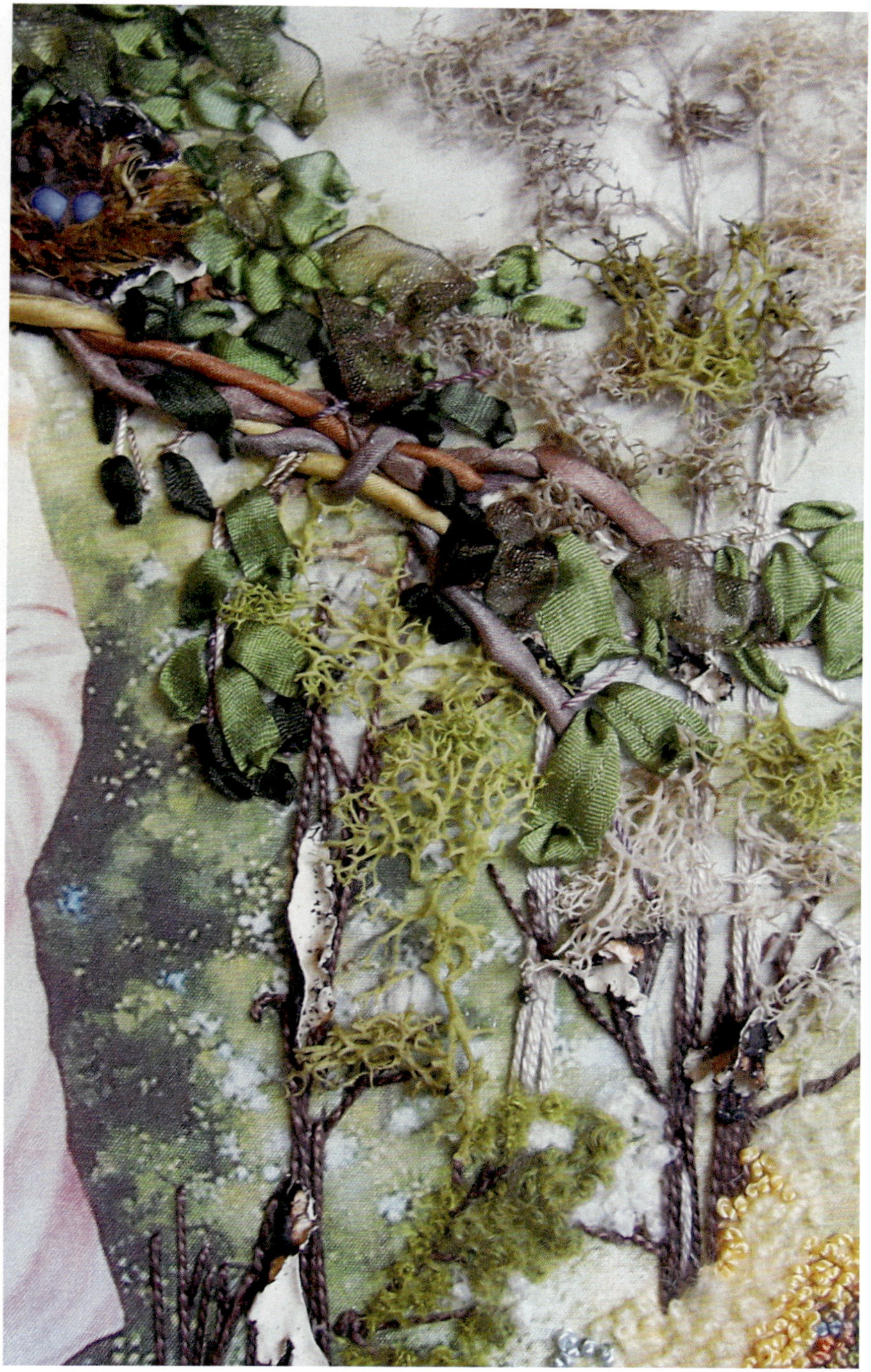

Claire Rubie
Brisbane, Queensland
Australia

"Although I have participated in several crafts over the years I did not find the world of embroidery until about 10 years ago and fell in love. I didn't know where to start but assumed if someone else could do it then so could I. My first efforts hang in my craft room as a reminder of where I started. Wanting to explore further, I began taking lessons, doing just about every form of embroidery I could, but my passion is making pictures come alive with what I call 3D embroidery through the use of stumpwork, trapunto, ribbon- and thread embroidery incorporating things such as mulberry bark, silk rods, water soley, stiffy and just about anything else that grabs my attention. I thoroughly enjoyed making my "girl reaching" come alive with each stitch as it reminded me of my granddaughters and how life is such an adventure."

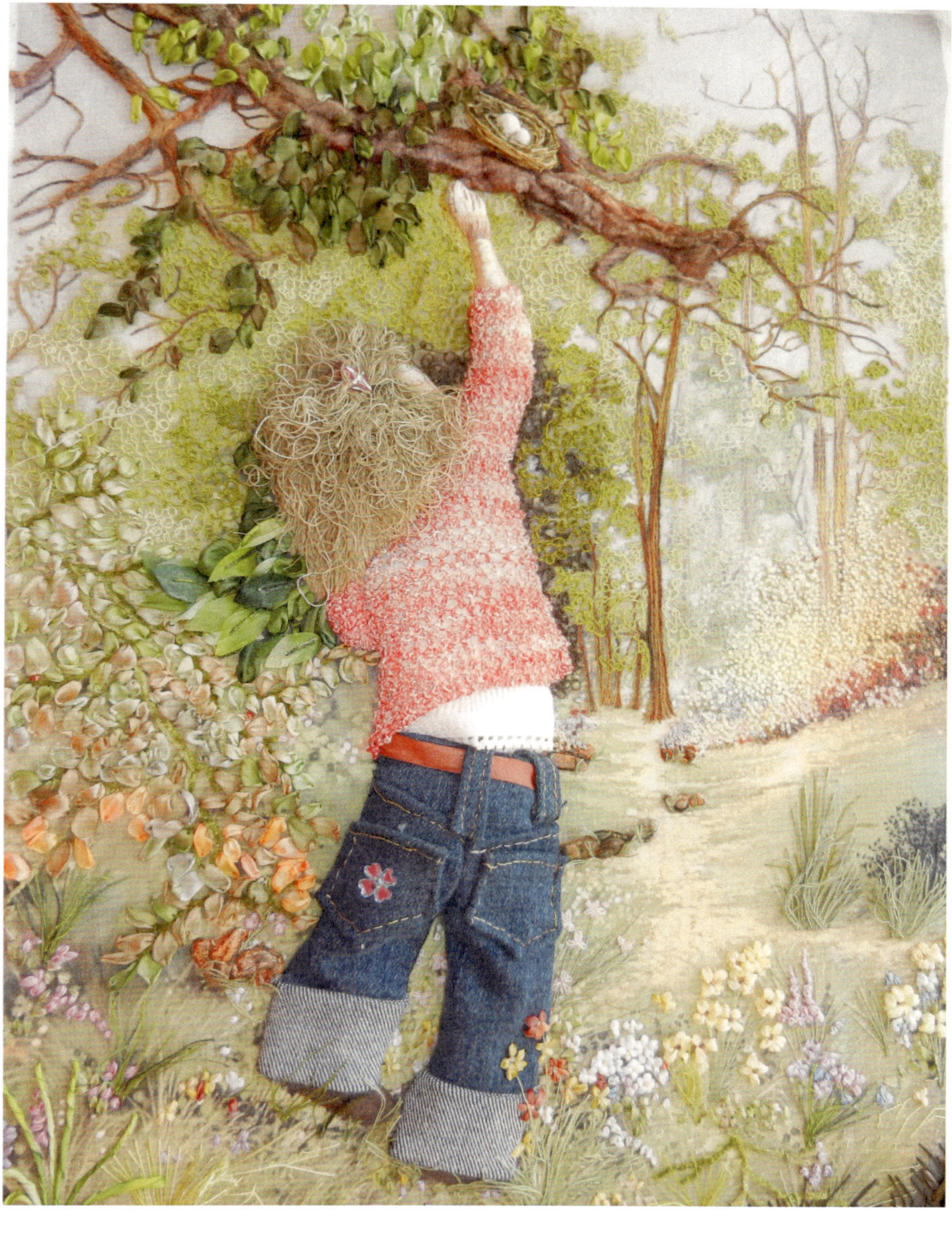

"For the tree trunks and branches in the background, working towards the foreground, use rows of stem stitches in accordance to the thickness of the branches. Make sure the branches in foreground are stitched over the ones in the background. The lighter green branches in the left foreground are done later. I like a 3D effect and find it important to do all elements in the distance first and gradually work forward.

For the middle sized branches, where the nest is, use bark from a paper tree or rows of textured yarn, fabric or fibre, in brown tonings and tease pieces about 1cm wide away from original piece. Don't be concerned about it being crooked. I then rolled it lengthwise and dampened them very slightly to assist with shaping. These are then stitched in place being careful to hide stitches where possible. Only put enough stitches to hold in place as too many will destroy the bark.

For the large branch, I used a silk rod in colours as close to bark colour as possible. I stretched this out lengthwise being careful not to tear it, until it is the required lenght. This is then stitched in place along the edge – this will form a tunnel – then stitch spasmodically through the centre section to distort and texturize the branch.

When this is finished, I did some more stitching to meld the smallest branches to the larger ones. Then I used aquarelle pencils or poster paint to add colour where needed to blend everything together – be very careful not to get any on the print.

Work the background leaves using 'one wrong' French knots, making sure not to stitch over the sky area as this gives depth to the picture.

Give thought as to which branches are in the foreground and which are covered by leaves. Once done, to give the illusion that the leaves between the trees are in the distance, I have cut a piece of white organza a little larger than the area I want covered and slip stitched it in place rolling the edges under. Then on the top I have repeated the French knots randomly near the edge to give even more depth. Stitch the leaves in the shadow close to the girl in the same manner. The stitching can also cover the raised arm of the girl. Make sure you have copied the outline of the girl before doing this.

Using between one and four wrap French knots in appropriate colours, work the flowers at the base of trees in the background.

For the leaves of the main branches use silk ribbon to form a mixture of straight and ribbon stitches making sure you use the brighter ribbon for where the light may catch and the darker for the leaves in the shadows.

Gently lift the leaves off the work, so they do not all seem flat against your work. You may want to do some work on the girl before completing this step as it may be easier to judge the perspective of the leaves better. Work the purple flowers with seed stitches.

Trace the jeans a little larger than needed to allow for seams and leg turnups and padding, just as you would for a pair of pants for yourself, then cut fabric of your choice. Next stitch together using either back stitch or a machine then attach to embroidery using slip stitch. I added a little more padding to the bottom area to give a better shape to the area.

Cut a small piece from an old baby singlet and poked it up under the jumper. I did put a light pink dye wash through it first to take the starkness of the white away, but this is up to you. For the belt I used ribbon and passed it through the pant loops and stitched down at the side. I also added a little bling to the back pocket.

For the hair I cut long lengths, about 1m, of thread and wound it around a shaft of a screwdriver and painted it with fabric stiffener and allowed to dry. I did 7–8 metres like this. When dry, gently unwind the thread. Before placing these curls on the hair do layers of straight stitch in the direction you want the hair to fall using this same but unstiffened thread. Thread a long length of curl and pass the needle up and back down again at the hairline leaving a loop the length of the hair. Allow for the spring of the curl.

Keep doing this until you have the coverage you want. These do not have to be secured as there will be no wear and tear when finished and the stiffness and curl keep them from falling out. Pull hair back gently and attach a bead or two to form a hair clip as desired. Us a few couching stitches to keep hair in place.

Using a selection of ribbons work a selection of French knots, ribbon stitch and straight stitches to make small flowers where appropriate putting a small French knot in the thread colour of choice in the centre of the larger flowers.

Using silk ribbon, make small straight stitches for the small green leaves on the ground in the front.

The stem of the branch on the left of the girl is done in a way that it is slightly raised from the work. Using silk ribbon work a mixture of ribbon and straight stitches. Using anti-fray agent, paint about 5cm of each of the ribbons used and cut into left shapes and stitch these into the leaves randomly.

The larger dark green leaves are done with ribbon or straight stitch. Once again use anti-fray agent on some of this ribbon then cut into leaf shapes when dry. Also wired veins can be attached to some to give a little more texture and interest if you like.

The grasses are done in a mix of any greens you think appropriate. I did straight stitches using a rough fan shape and couched bends into some of the stalks. I also used some very loose straight and turkey stitches to give dimension.

The grasses on the right are done using double threads using straight stitch and couch into position. On top of this work straight stitch, slightly twisted with ribbon and couched into position. For the detached grasses, use thin wire and fold in half and weave back and forth. Attach randomly across front.

The next is made by wrapping straw or raffia in a circle and gluing and stitching into shape. I then coloured it using Inktense pencil colours. The eggs are beads covered with ribbon and attached to inside of nest."

112

PART 14

Olive owl

Lena Thiel
Marina Zherdeva

Lena Thiel
Vasteras, Sweden

"My name is Lena Thiel and I live in Sweden with my family. I have always been working with my hands. After school I went for Art education here in Sweden, and also followed a two year distance course at OPUS School of Art, London, England.

I work with many different handicraft techniques of which silk ribbon embroidery is one. I enjoy to mix different techniques in my work. I also like sewing, crochet teddy bears, making dolls, make creations with pearls and free machine embroidery.

My inspiration comes from everywhere and from anything.

It can be something I see in a paper or on the Internet. But also when I visit exhibitions or fairs. This picture of me was taken in my garden.

The first time I found out about silk ribbon embroidery was some time around 1995. It was a shop here in Sweden that presented ribbon embroidery courses. I attended over weekends, and after that I have often done embroidery."

"For this challenge I chose to do the olive owl, but I wanted to make something special, so I've decided to do the embroidery on a felted IPAD case, which I also made myself.

I used merino wool roving in different colours and made the felted pieces using hot water and soap. First I made a simple sketch to plan my project.

I made a special pocket on the front of the case, where I could place the owl and sew him to the IPAD case.

I used mostly silk ribbon to embroider and create my owl."

115

iPad case

FRONT → BACK ← FRONT

FRONT

SILK RIBBONS
- 2mm 86
- " 103
- 4mm 26
- " 51
- " 77
- " 80
- " 82
- " 90
- " 91
- " 99
- 7mm 79
- " 103
- " 117

DMC embroidery threads
- 754
- 3774
- 225
- 3348
- 372
- 758
- 310
- 606

LenaT 2012

117

Marina Zherdeva
Moscow, Russia

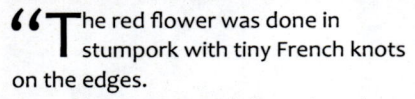

"The red flower was done in stumpork with tiny French knots on the edges.

I worked long French knots in red on the inside of the ears. The eyebrows are made with a long twisted ribbon stitch.

I embroidered the stave on the music sheet with straight stitches.

For the forehead of the owl I dipped the yellow ribbon in water stabilizer solution or dabbed it with a glue stick on the reverse side of the ribbon. Let it dry, iron and cut out scallop shapes to create the look of feathers.

Divide the ribbons in different colour strips. Attach the ribbon strips to the design with small stitches, starting at the top of the owl's head.

Every next row overlaps the previous one and is slightly displaced.

For the owl's chest I used the same method as for the forehead to create the look of feathers on a bird's chest. Overlapping the piece will give the chest a raised effect.

The olive branches are made with twisted stitches. Some of the leaves are embroidered with straight ribbon stitch and others are cut out from the ribbon with a long tail, which is inserted into the panel on the back side and fixed with thread.

The wings are made with reversed double ribbon stitches and extended French knots.

The leaves are worked with straight double ribbon stitches; the branches with twisted stitches.

The legs are made with loose straight stitches. The eyes are a special element of the design and are embroidered separately.

I used the same metallic gold thread for the stave to embroider lines on the eyes.

Cut out the eyes, leaving a 5mm edge. Fold in the edges and attach the eye pieces to the design with small stitches. Before sewing it closed, fill the opening with stuffing to give the eye more volume and a raised effect. Attach a shiny bead onto the eye to add sparkle. The nose is sculptured using the papier-mâché method."

119

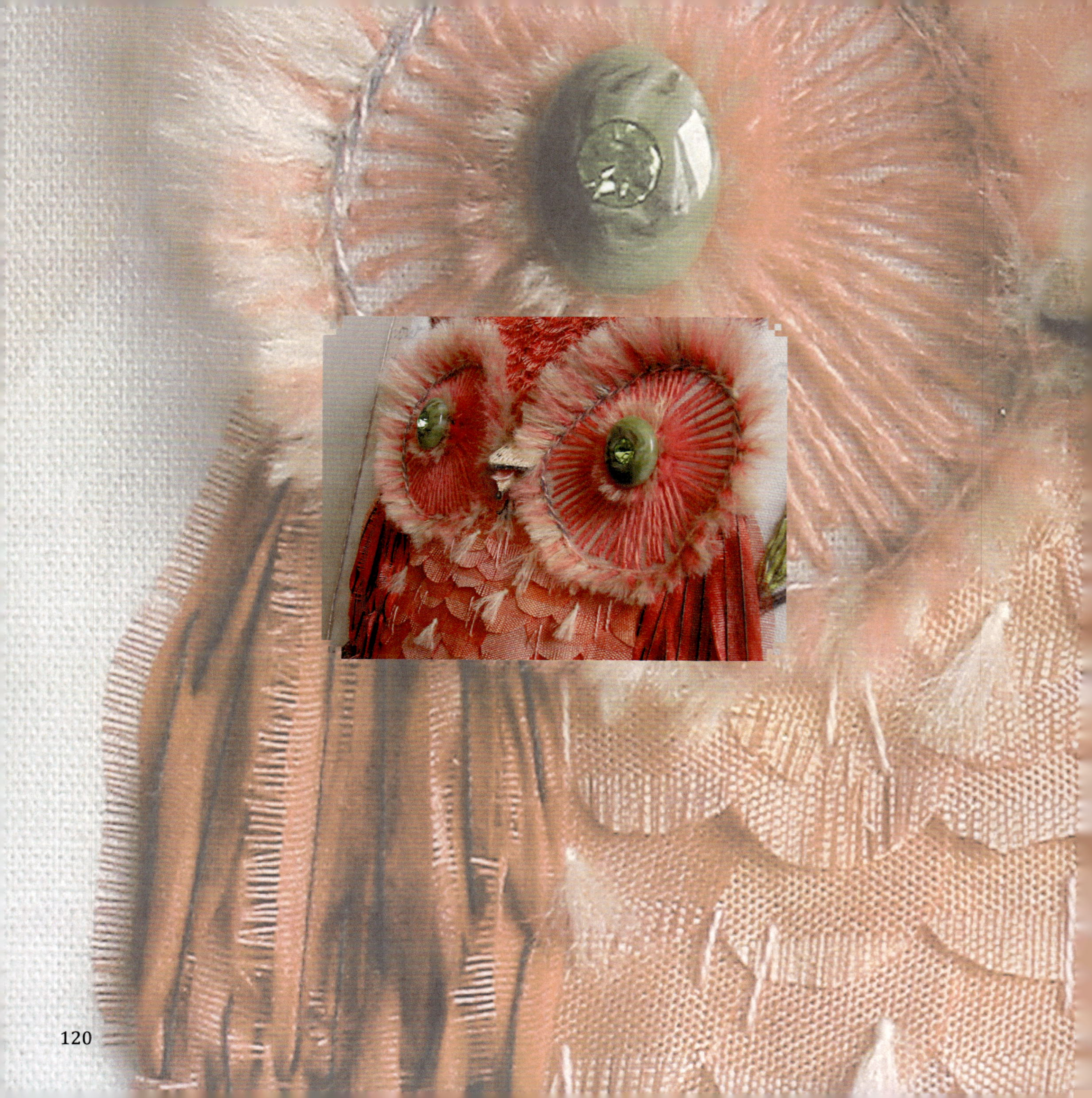

PART 15

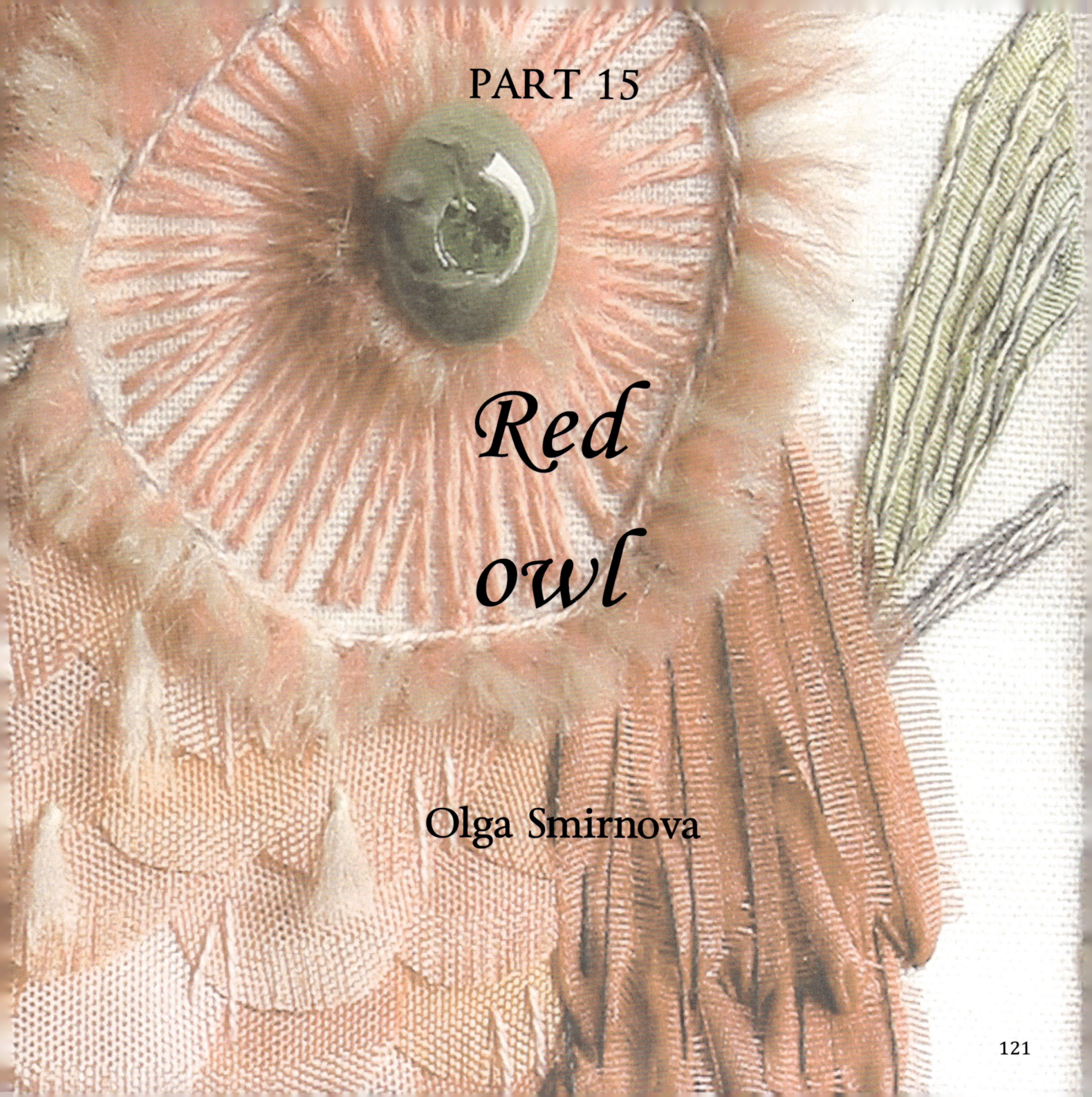

Red owl

Olga Smirnova

Olga Smirnova
St Petersburg, Russia

"I wanted the owl to be fluffy. Achieving this was quite a challenge. My idea was to cut the ribbon in half lengthways – splitting the ribbon – then unravel the raw edges, almost halfway, and as a result, create a ribbon with a frayed, shaggy edge. I used these ribbons to cover and embroider the owl's head and wings.

The beak is created and embroidered separately.

For the eyes I used two buttons with crystal bead inlays. These were ideal to give the owl bright, expressive eyes. My husband suggested that I use these buttons – which I did.

For the feathers on the owl's chest, cut a length of 13mm silk ribbon up into squares. Cut the one side, with raw edge, into a scallop shape to make the piece look like scales. Place the pieces onto the chest area, also like scales, and attach to the background with small slip stitches.

I decided to make a finder ring for the owl to stress that he is absolutely unique. I attached it to one of his toes.

On the design the owl is sitting on an olive branch with olives, but I really didn't like their appearance. I decided to make a magic fruit instead by making balls from nylon which I stuffed with batting and covered with sheer stretch fabric."

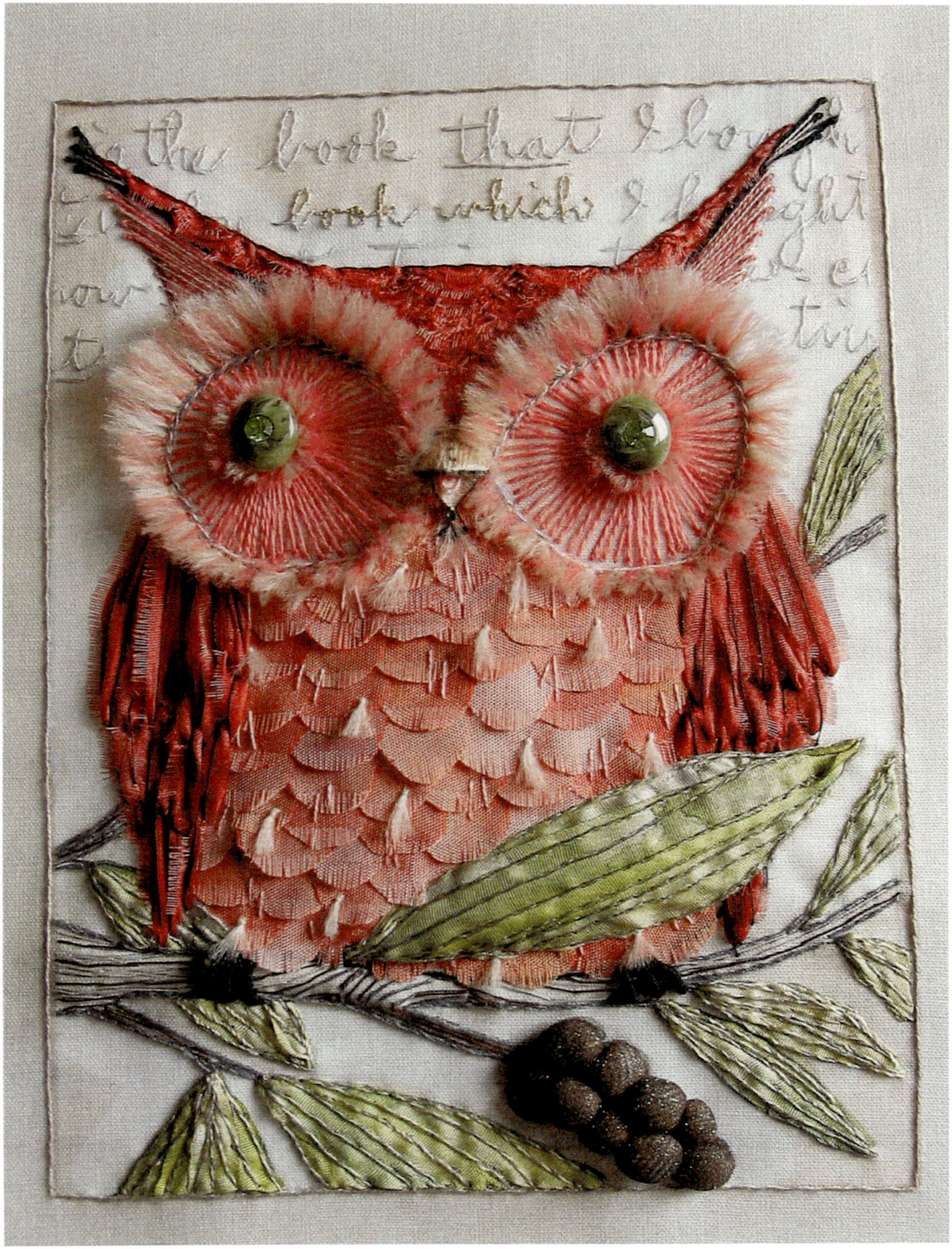
the book that
book which

124

125

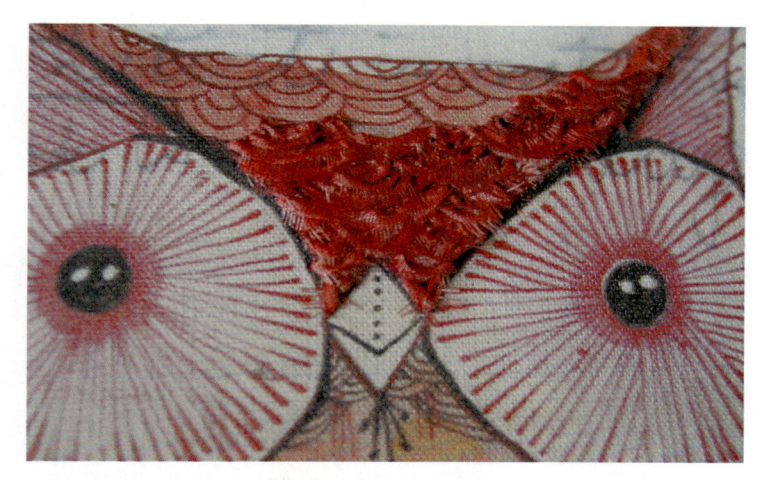

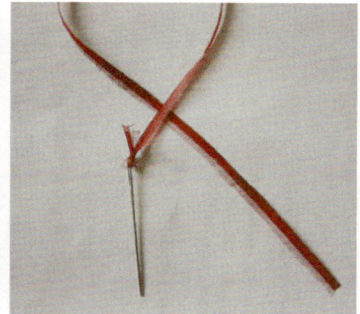

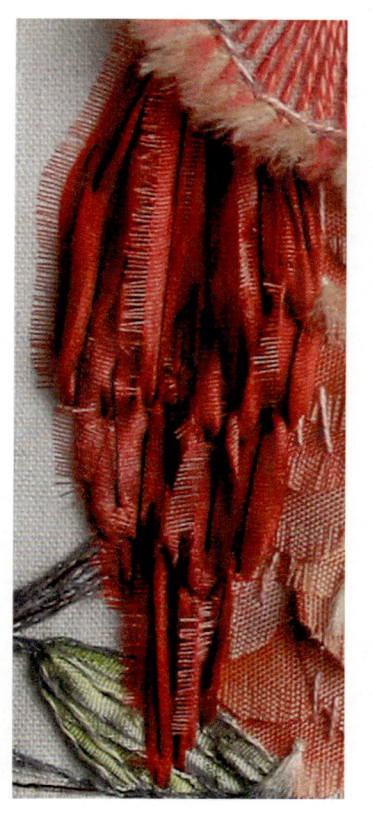

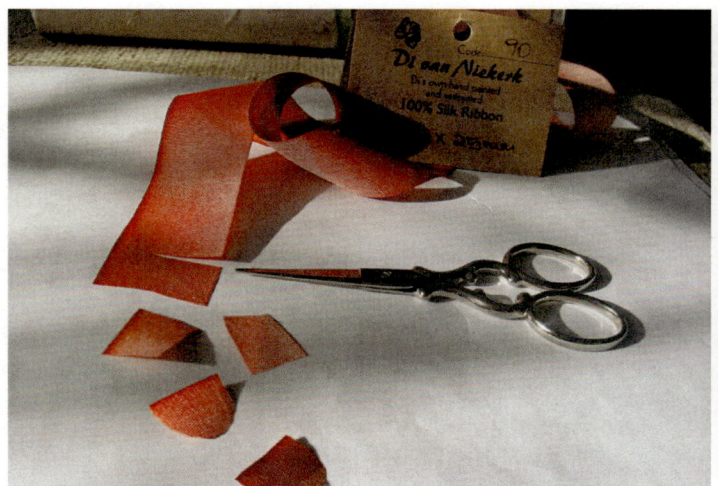

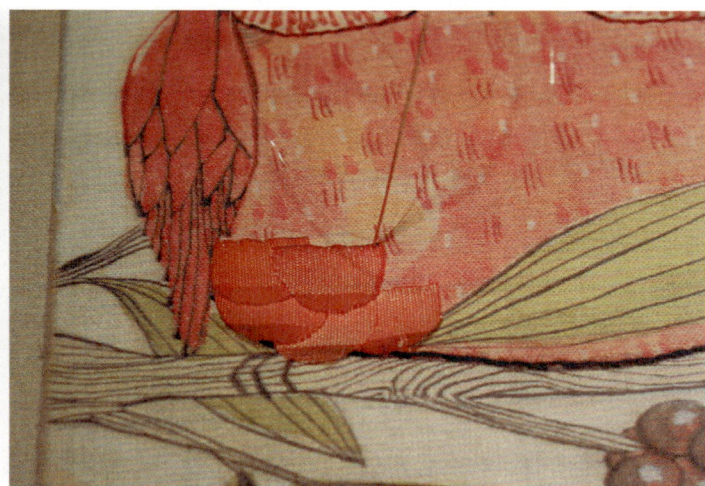

126

PART 16

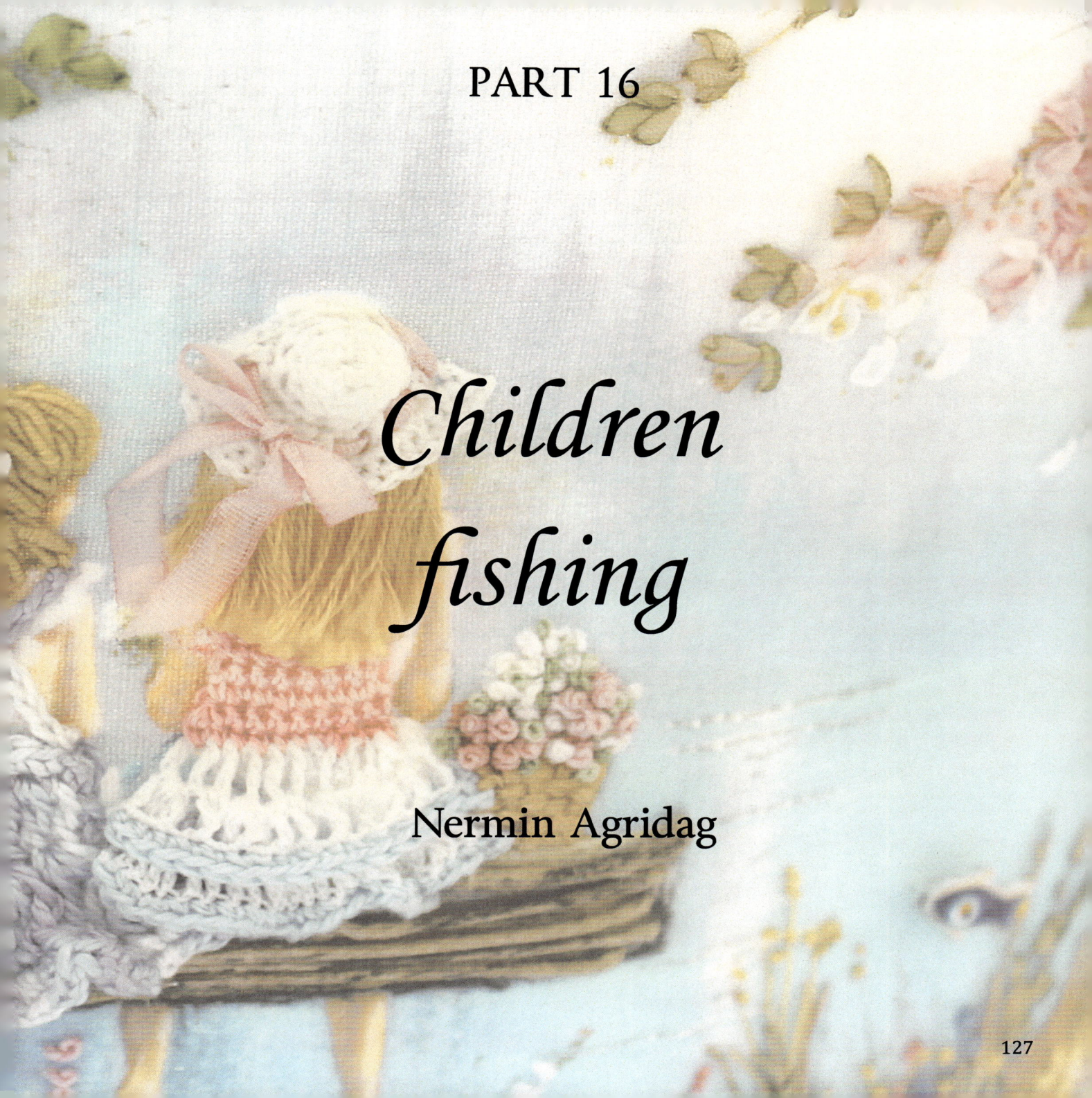

Children fishing

Nermin Agridag

Nermin Ağridağ
Bursa, Turkey

" I was born in Bursa, Turkey, in 1957. I am married and have a daughter. For fifteen years I attended courses on lace, accessories and jewellery, knitting, painting, flowers, patchwork and miniature in public training centres. I also worked as a teacher in these centers for ten years. I am currently teaching at a private institution of arts. I am really passionate about patchwork and ribbon embroidery. Not only do I love patchwork and embroidery, but I also believe that they are soothing and refreshing for us.

What I liked most about the kit are the tree and girls' dresses. I really like to make a combination of fabric, dye, lace and ribbons and add something from me, myself when I am working. I have been working on ribbon embroidery for seven years. In addition, I read and follow embroidery books, which I think includes really beautiful and nice examples."

"I used tricot fabric for the tree trunk and stones. I attached the tricot fabric to the tree trunk and coloured it with fabric dye. Then I worked on the thin branches. I knitted the girls' dresses and made patchwork clothes for the fisher boy. Silk ribbons stand out amongst other various materials used. I made the flowers and leaves with the ribbons I chose. I decided to turn the fisher boy kit into a lampshade. As the kit was rather small, I enriched it with a patchwork fabric with clouds and lace with a flamingo which I knitted with cotton perlé thread. I made trees where the lace and the fabric meet. I stuck this piece to the lampshade by using the white of an egg. For the butterfly I wrapped stuffing in a piece of organza fabric and used buttonhole to stitch around the edges. The lampshade fringe was made with cotton perlé thread and beads. The lace was knitted with cotton perlé for the major parts of the lampshade and coloured with fabric dye."

129

130

131

132

PART 17

Sunflowers and white roses

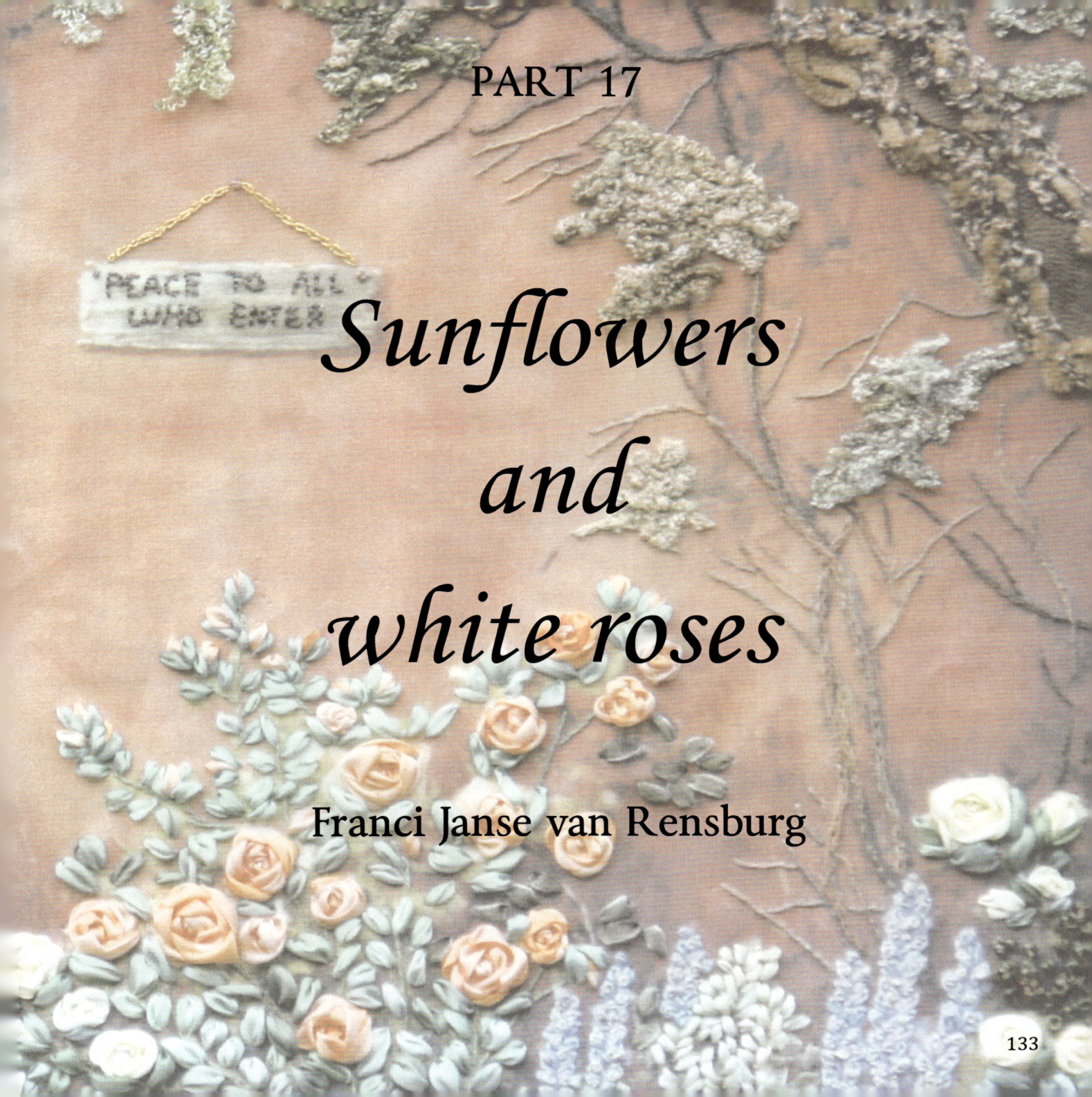

Franci Janse van Rensburg

Franci Janse van Rensburg
Pretoria, South Africa

"I was a teacher for 28 years and live in Pretoria. I have four most wonderful children, two boys and two girls. I am very proud of them and thank them for my eight beautiful grandchildren. When we moved to Pretoria it was my chance to find someone to teach me ribbon embroidery. A new world opened for me as I walked into Thyme Embroidery Studio and Viv Trent's warm welcome! In her gentle and encouraging way she introduced me to ribbon embroidery.

My inspiration for the project was the door and the invitation of the sunflowers.

I enjoyed every stitch of my project. I always had the desire to do ribbon embroidery and have now grabbed the opportunity to do so. All I can say is: I love it, I love it, I love it!"

135

137